kamera
BOOKS

www.kamerabooks.com

Douglas Keesey

NEO-NOIR

First published in 2010 by Kamera Books
PO Box 394, Harpenden, Herts, AL5 1XJ
www.kamerabooks.com

Copyright © Douglas Keesey 2010
Series Editor: Hannah Patterson

The right of Douglas Keesey to be identified as the author of this work has been asserted in accordance with the Copyright, Designs and Patents Act 1988.

All rights reserved. No part of this book may be reproduced, stored in or introduced into a retrieval system, or transmitted, in any form or by any means (electronic, mechanical, photocopying, recording or otherwise) without the written permission of the publishers.

Any person who does any unauthorised act in relation to this publication may be liable to criminal prosecution and civil claims for damages.

A CIP catalogue record for this book is available from the British Library.

ISBN 978-1-84243-311-9

2 4 6 8 10 9 7 5 3 1

Typeset by Elsa Mathern
Printed and bound in Great Britain by JF Print, Sparkford, Somerset

ACKNOWLEDGEMENTS

I am grateful to Hannah Patterson for her faith in this project from the beginning and for all her wonderful advice on the way to its completion. Linda Halisky, David Kann, Steven Marx and Kathryn Rummell helped provide me with a sabbatical along with travel and research funds which proved vital to sustaining this work. I am lucky to have benefited from stimulating conversations about film with Damon Bailey, Cameron Bowman, Kevin Clark, Jack Conroy, George Cotkin, Bill Covey, Michael Flores, William Frederick, David Gillette, John Hampsey, John Harrington, Brenda Helmbrecht, Scott Keesey, Carol MacCurdy, Andy Maness, Paul Marchbanks, Cheryl Ney, Tom O'Brien, Todd Pierce, Johanna Rubba, Mark Stablein, Glen Starkey and Patricia Troxel. My special thanks to Jim Dee for screening neo-noirs for my film students at the Palm Theater. I owe a huge debt of gratitude to Cal Poly's marvellous support staff; their prompt, professional and patient help has made all the difference to me: Katie Tool, Connie Davis, Sue Otto, Kathy Severn and Margie Valine in the administrative offices; Karen Beaton, Judy Drake, Linda Hauck, Jan Kline, Nancy Loe, Heather Lucio, José Montelongo, Holly Richmond, and Janice Stone in the library; Daniel Barnicle, Tom Dresel, Jennifer Hodges, Daniel Park and Velanche Stewart of the CLA Tech Team. My parents, Donald and Phyllis Keesey, continue to be an inspiration to me in so many ways. Finally, I am grateful to my wife, Helen Bailey, without whose company I would never have ventured to go 'down these mean streets'.

CONTENTS

Introduction	9
Neo-Noir Landmarks	19
Neo-Noir Auteurs	51
Neo-Noir Discoveries	117
Neo-Noir International	131
Neo-Noir Remakes	155
Recommended Films for Further Viewing	195
Bibliography	201
Notes	205
Index	211

INTRODUCTION

'I'm a bad girl,' says Laure (Rebecca Romijn) in *Femme Fatale*, 'real bad – rotten to the heart.' Laure *knows* that she's a femme fatale. In fact, she just watched *Double Indemnity* on TV and is modelling her behaviour after that of the lovely but lethal Barbara Stanwyck in that film. In *Basic Instinct*, writer Catherine Tramell (Sharon Stone) tells detective Nick Curran (Michael Douglas) that her book is about 'a detective. He falls for the wrong woman. She kills him.' They both know that this is the plot of many classic film noirs – and *we* know that they know and are intrigued to discover whether their story will turn out the same. 'This isn't going to have a happy ending,' Somerset (Morgan Freeman) tells Mills (Brad Pitt) in *Se7en*, for Somerset is conscious of the role they are playing in the kind of noirish tale that almost always has a dark conclusion. ('Film noir' is French for 'dark movie' – with 'dark' meaning 'sinister' and 'dreadful' as well as 'shadowy', as in Raymond Chandler's great line, 'The streets were dark with something more than night.')[1] Contemporary film noir, or neo-noir, is a highly self-conscious genre, keenly aware of the plot conventions, character types and common techniques associated with past film noirs. Indeed, some neo-noirs are actually about scripting or acting in noir films (*The Singing Detective*, *Bad Education*, *INLAND EMPIRE*), while other neo-noirs are remakes of classic film noirs (*The Postman Always Rings Twice*) or 'retro-noir' homages set in the period of, and consciously styled after, past noir films (*Chinatown*, *Body Heat*, *L.A. Confidential*, *The Man Who Wasn't There*).

The time span of classic film noir is often said to stretch from *The Maltese Falcon* (1941) to *Touch of Evil* (1958). Although they had some growing awareness of genre conventions, the makers of the great 1940s and '50s noir movies – *Double Indemnity, Laura, Detour, The Postman Always Rings Twice, D.O.A., Sunset Blvd., Kiss Me Deadly, The Killing* and *Vertigo* – did not conceive of them as a single genre of 'film noirs'. Instead, these movies were known by a variety of different labels, including 'crime stories', 'suspense pictures', 'psychological thrillers' and 'melodramas'. It was French critics, particularly Raymond Borde and Etienne Chaumeton in their 1955 book *A Panorama of American Film Noir*, who first popularised the term 'film noir', noting that several of these movies were based on the hardboiled detective fiction and crime novels of Raymond Chandler, Dashiell Hammett and James M Cain, which had been published in France under the imprint 'Série Noire' (meaning 'a dark series of books' but also punning on 'a series of bad events'). As the study of this newly recognised genre took off among British and American critics in the 1970s, the roots of film noir were traced to German Expressionist, French Poetic Realist, and Hollywood gangster films of the 1920s and '30s. In addition to these cinematic precursors, the biggest historical influences were identified as World War II and the ensuing Cold War, with the violence of combat, the threat of nuclear destruction and the 'red scares' of McCarthyism spreading paranoia, rage and disillusionment – all emotions characteristic of film noir. The femme fatale – seducer and betrayer of the hapless hero – was also seen as springing from a post-war change in the balance of power between the sexes: male veterans, physically and psychically wounded in the war, came home to find that women had grown in financial and sexual independence from having joined the workforce as part of the home-front war effort. Men found such powerful women both alluring and frightening – the same ambivalence felt for the femme fatale. Techniques that have been identified as typical of film noir include dark shadows, particularly those that fall in chiaroscuro patterns like bars or spiders' webs, seeming to entrap the hero; oppressive, angle-down shots and claustrophobic framings; distorting mirrors and unbalanced compositions; and flashbacks and voiceover narration that give visual and aural emphasis to the personal traumas experienced by the disoriented and doomed hero.

And yet, despite the many efforts to describe it, film noir remains the most disputed of all movie genres. Critics disagree about whether there is any one defining element common to all film noirs and about which movies fit and which should be excluded from the genre. As James Naremore points out, 'There are many themes, moods, characters, locales, and stylistic features associated with noir, no one of which is shared by all the films that have been placed in the category.'[2] Not all noirs have a detective-hero, or a femme fatale, or even a tragic ending. Should heist movies, or gangster films, or female Gothic melodramas be categorised as film noirs? In this book, I follow the lead of recent critics who have argued for an expansive understanding of film noir. According to Wheeler Winston Dixon, 'most definitions of noir films are, it seems to me, excessively narrow. The classic archetypes of the lone protagonist in a dark, rainy alley, accompanied by an omnipresent voiceover on the soundtrack, of doomed lovers on the run from the police, or hardboiled detectives unravelling labyrinthian mysteries with cynical assurance, represent only one manifestation of this pervasive film genre.'[3] Jim Hillier and Alastair Phillips contend that 'film noir is as much about a state of mind as a single set of stylistic signs' and that 'there is no such thing perhaps as a film noir but rather many forms and variations of a sensibility that alters and shifts according to culture, place and time'.[4]

Which brings us to neo-noir. If defining classic film noir is difficult, the challenge only increases with contemporary film noir. Since, as Mark Bould rightly observes, 'each additional film noir rethinks, reconstructs and refabricates the genre',[5] are there any useful generalisations that can be made about films as diverse as *The Crying Game*, *Reservoir Dogs*, *The Matrix* and *Memento*? My claim is that, in addition to being highly self-conscious of their relation to past noirs, neo-noirs are characterised by blurred boundaries and hybrid genres, and that what is new about neo-noirs can be traced to the influence of contemporary social changes and historical events as well as the latest trends and technological advances in filmmaking.

Blurred Boundaries

Many classic film noirs consist of three character types: the investigator, the villain and the victim. While even past noirs put some pressure on the boundaries between these types, neo-noir really tends to erode these distinctions. In *The French Connection*, 'Popeye' Doyle (Gene Hackman) is a zealous cop whose reckless disregard for the law may help him to catch crooks but also threatens to make him one of them, as this film points to 'the thin line between the policeman and the criminal' which is 'very often crossed over'.[6] In *Manhunter*, Will Graham (William Petersen) is an FBI profiler who must think like the monstrous murderer he seeks – but not too much like him. As the film's tagline warns, 'Enter the mind of a serial killer... you may never come back.' The undercover cop (Leonardo DiCaprio) and the gangster mole (Matt Damon) in *The Departed* are affected by their assumed identities and become morally ambiguous characters: 'No one knows who they really are, or who anyone else really is.'[7] More and more, the difference *between* the investigator and the villain comes to seem like a difference *within* the investigator, who, if he looks hard enough, may find the potential for evil inside himself. 'You don't know who you are anymore,' Leonard (Guy Pearce) is told in *Memento*. 'Maybe it's time you started investigating yourself.' Similarly, a new psychological understanding of the femme fatale may reveal that her 'evil' is really the result of her having been abused, that she is actually more victim than villain, as can be seen in *Blade Runner*, *The Crying Game*, *Devil in a Blue Dress* and *Bad Education*. In neo-noir, villainous females can break out of the stereotype to become investigator-heroes (as in *Femme Fatale* and *INLAND EMPIRE*), but female investigators can also be morally compromised to the point of villainy (see *Blue Steel* and *demonlover*). Finally, male investigators are more likely to end up as victims in neo-noir, not only because the villains are too strong for them but because the investigators themselves are morally compromised – so complicit that they have already lost part of the battle. Even in classic film noir, the detective was often beaten up and tempted by sin on the way to solving the case and catching the killer, but the investigations in neo-noir can end in pyrrhic victory or outright failure, with the hero himself becoming just another victim (see *Chinatown*, *Reservoir Dogs*, *Se7en*, *Following* and *Basic Instinct 2*).

Hybrid Genres

Already in the 1940s and '50s, noir was having an influence on other kinds of films, creating hybrid genres such as noir melodramas (*Possessed*), noir westerns (*Blood on the Moon*), noir gangster sagas (*White Heat*), noir science fiction (*Invasion of the Body Snatchers*) and even noir musicals (*The Band Wagon*). But, by the time of neo-noir, it sometimes seems as though noir has spread into virtually all other genres, and with noir has come a troubling of the clear-cut distinctions that used to be maintained within each genre. In the traditional police procedural (such as TV's *Dragnet* [1951–59]), the cops are clearly the good guys tracking down the evildoers, but in the noir-influenced *Dexter* (2006–) the man in the crime lab is himself a serial killer, blurring the line between pursuer and pursued, moral and immoral. The anti-hero of the classic gangster film always inspired a mixture of attraction and repulsion in the viewer, but this is nothing compared to the moral ambivalence we feel towards Tony Soprano (James Gandolfini) in *The Sopranos* (1999–2007), who is psychoanalysed, leading us to confront both the good and the bad in him. Traditional romances and comedies often take place in idyllic small towns or natural settings, as opposed to classic film noirs whose terrible events unfold in the big bad city. But in neo-noirs like *Blood Simple*, *Blue Velvet*, *Fargo* and *The Talented Mr. Ripley*, the city/country distinction breaks down as crime and corruption are shown to be present even in sunny climes ('white noir') and agrarian locales ('country noir'). In 'techno-noirs' such as *Blade Runner* and *The Matrix*, noir's pessimism invades science fiction to imagine near-futures where the hope for human advancement through science has been turned into a dystopian nightmare. And 'superhero noirs' reveal the moral doubts and failings of those who, in earlier incarnations, were simply our saviours. In *The Dark Knight*, a vengeful Batman struggles to differentiate himself from the vengeful Joker, while in *Watchmen* some of the vigilante superheroes prove hard to distinguish from the villains, leading a fearful populace to wonder, 'Who watches the Watchmen?'

Contemporary Social Changes and Historical Events

Writer/director Paul Schrader has said that 'as a filmmaker you look for rips and tears in the social fabric that can be addressed metaphorically'.[8] There are some neo-noirs in which the traumatic impact of contemporary events is not difficult to decode. *Taxi Driver* is about a Vietnam veteran in the urban jungle of New York City who has trouble telling friend from foe and who commits a massacre, destroying a 'village' in order to save it. *Chinatown*, though set in the 1930s, reflects the widespread suspicion of rampant corruption among supposedly benign authority figures that followed upon the Watergate scandal. More recently, the remake of *The Manchurian Candidate* exposes the trumped-up xenophobia manufactured by war-profiteering corporations, while *The Dark Knight* shows a populace tempted to turn against and destroy itself as a result of Bush-era fear-mongering about terrorism.

With other neo-noirs, it is less a case of specific historical events and more a matter of larger social changes that have had an influence.

The women's movement and the male backlash against it have deepened audience ambivalence towards the femme fatale. More women today are empowered in the bedroom and the workplace, and there is a tendency to cheer the femme fatales in *Body Heat*, *Basic Instinct* and *Bound* as they seek their own pleasure and profit – and often get away with both in the end. But these women also embody male fears of sexually liberated women as castrating predators and of independent career women as out to steal men's money. The abolition of Hays Code censorship restrictions, along with the introduction of an age-appropriate ratings system, has led to a new frankness of female nudity and sexually explicit speech, but here again neo-noir's representation of woman tends to be ambiguous: is her open sexuality to be celebrated or feared as overly aggressive? Is her own desire being encouraged or will she be reduced to an object of the voyeuristic male gaze? Feminism has also prompted men to question their own investment in machismo, and many neo-noirs are deeply split in their attitude to the 'hardboiled hero' – both admiring and critical. In *The Samurai*, *Pulp Fiction*, *Ichi the Killer* and *I'll Sleep When I'm Dead*, being a tough guy is shown to be both cool and self-destructive, while the macho killers in *Fingers*, *The Crying Game* and *Amores Perros* struggle to find a way to admit their sensitive sides without feeling emasculated. The gay rights and civil rights movements have brought a new complexity to neo-noirs like *Cruising* and *Suture* where the white hetero hero's struggle turns out to be with his own repressed homosexual side or with the 'black brother' whom he has oppressed.

In addition to issues of gender, sexuality and race, social tensions related to class have had a major impact on contemporary film noir. The 'greed is good' mentality of the Thatcher, Reagan and Bush years can be seen in the selfish scheming of the characters in *Body Heat*, *Blood Simple*, *Fargo* and *Following*, who are all the more driven to emulate the rapacious greed of the upper classes by the fact that the disparity between the very rich and the very poor has grown ever wider. The satisfaction we may feel in seeing these selfish, low-life characters come to a bad end is complicated by a sense of how unjust it is that they should have so little when others – who are no more deserving – have so much. The materialistic mindset of our conservative politicians and corporate leaders is also evident in the lust for high-priced commodities, which plays such a large part in the desire – and often the downfall – of the characters in *To Live and Die in L.A.*, *The Talented Mr. Ripley*, *The Departed* and *Basic Instinct 2*. The increasing ability of corporations to use the media as a way of manipulating what we desire as consumers – and even what we believe to be real – has fed the paranoia and pessimism of such techno-noirs as *Blade Runner*, *The Matrix*, *Vanilla Sky* and *demonlover*.

Trends and Technological Advances in Filmmaking

Stylistically, neo-noir owes a great debt to the film movement known as the French New Wave, exemplified by the late-1950s and early-'60s films of Jean-Luc Godard and François Truffaut with their mobile camerawork (including hand-held tracking shots), experimental editing (freeze frames and jump cuts), outdoor shooting and (sometimes parodic) self-awareness of genres. Many of these innovative techniques were adopted by New Hollywood directors (Robert Altman, Brian De Palma, Martin Scorsese) and went on to influence the makers of contemporary film noir. Technological advances affecting the look of neo-noir include the development of faster film stock and then of digital video, enabling on-location scenes to be shot in colour under low-light conditions (and also allowing high-contrast images with truer blacks to be obtained even on colour film). The increasing use of widescreen composition aided in the presentation of neo-noir characters being enveloped by darkness (see *Lost Highway*) or surrounded by a vast emptiness (as in the 'white noir' *Point Blank*). The invention of the Steadicam helped us to move with and physically experience events alongside the neo-noir hero, and the development of digital editing has made it easier to convey that hero's disorientation through accelerated cutting and through flashback images that break in as shock cuts. Multilayered voices and effects on the soundtrack, combined with music that tends towards dissonance and unresolved harmonies, have worked to dramatise the psychological complexity and moral ambiguity of the neo-noir protagonist. And CGI images and other digital effects have presented a neo-noir world that seems ever more threatening and unreliable, constantly morphing under the control of shadowy others – or because of the hero's own unstable mind.

This book covers 69 films, which are grouped into the following sections: neo-noirs that have made the biggest splash in the field ('landmarks'); films by directors who have become cult figures of neo-noir ('auteurs'); neo-noirs that deal with age, gender, race and sexuality ('discoveries'); neo-noirs from non-English-speaking countries ('international') and neo-noirs that put a new spin on past noirs ('remakes'). For each film, the title and date of release are given, followed by the names of the crew: director, writer, producer, editor and cinematographer. The key members of the cast are then listed, matched to the names of the characters they play. A fairly detailed plot summary of each film is supplied, followed by my own comments on the meaning of the film. Wherever possible, I have tried to add to the already existing scholarship by providing original insights and provoking the reader to new ways of thinking about each film. For some films, there are also 'factoids' that present intriguing facts, behind-the-scenes anecdotes and quotes from the cast and crew. The book concludes with a list of recommended films for further viewing, along with a bibliography of books on neo-noir for further reading. An index of names and film titles is provided to help readers locate these quickly in the text.

NEO-NOIR LANDMARKS

Chinatown (1974)

Directed by: Roman Polanski
Written by: Robert Towne
Produced by: Robert Evans
Edited by: Sam O'Steen
Cinematography: John A Alonzo
Cast: Jack Nicholson (*JJ 'Jake' Gittes*), Faye Dunaway (*Evelyn Mulwray*), John Huston (*Noah Cross*)

Plot

Los Angeles, 1937. Private eye Jake Gittes is hired by Evelyn Mulwray to get photographic evidence that her husband Hollis is being unfaithful. However, after these pictures of Hollis in the company of a younger woman are published in the newspaper, Jake realises that he has been duped: the woman who hired him was a fake, and Jake's photos were used to discredit Hollis who, as chief water engineer, was opposed to building a dam he felt would be unsafe. Then, when Hollis is found drowned, the real Evelyn Mulwray hires Jake to find out who did it and why. It turns out that Hollis may have been killed because he uncovered a conspiracy to dump fresh water into the ocean, buy up cheap land and then make a fortune when a dam is built and that land becomes water-rich. Jake suspects that Hollis's former business partner and Evelyn's father, Noah Cross, may be behind the conspiracy and Hollis's murder. However, Cross throws suspicion upon Evelyn, whom he describes as a dangerously jealous woman. Could she have killed Hollis, and what might she do to the younger woman Hollis was seen with? Cross hires Jake to find this younger woman. Jake wants to believe in Evelyn's innocence – the two of them even make love – but he is also afraid that she has seduced him so that he won't suspect her. When Jake finds the younger woman at Evelyn's house, he slaps Evelyn around to get her to talk, and she reveals that the younger woman (Katherine) is both her sister and her daughter – the product of incest between Cross and Evelyn. Jake confronts Cross with the fact that his glasses were found in the fish pond where Hollis drowned: Cross killed him because Hollis was trying to keep Cross from getting to Katherine. However, Cross forces Jake to give him back the incriminating glasses and to take him to Chinatown, where Jake has arranged to meet Evelyn and Katherine to help them escape. Police handcuff Jake to another cop, so he can do nothing but watch helplessly as events take their course. When Cross tries to take Katherine, Evelyn shoots him in the shoulder and attempts to drive off with Katherine in the car. But a warning shot from a policeman's gun accidentally kills Evelyn, and Cross claims Katherine in the end.

Comments

In this neo-noir, the detective solves the crime but fails to save the woman he had tried to protect. Moreover, the criminal goes unpunished, free to grab more land and more women, extending his illegal enterprise unchecked into the future. For Jake, this disastrous case seems like a repetition of a past time when he tried 'to keep someone from being hurt' and only 'ended up making sure that she was hurt'. Jake not only fails to prevent Evelyn from being hurt, he is complicit in what happens to her. Perhaps because Jake was fooled by the fake Evelyn, he is wary of being duped again. Cross feeds

Jake's suspicion that Evelyn may be a femme fatale, and Jake even physically abuses her, making us wonder how different he really is from Cross. Jake's vanity as a detective leads him to persist in trying to solve Hollis's murder no matter what the consequences, and to foolishly confront Cross, enabling Cross to take back his glasses (the only evidence against him) and to locate the woman he wants to victimise (Jake takes Cross right to Katherine!). Like Oedipus, Jake discovers that he is complicit in the crime he has been investigating. According to writer Robert Towne, 'All detective stories are a re-telling of the Oedipus tale. I mean those… movies where the detective is looking for the solution… [and] finds he's part of the crime, that he's part of the problem.'[9] It's tempting to argue that everyone might have benefited if this detective had never sought to find out the truth. As Jake himself warns a client early on, 'You're better off not knowing.' Evelyn is shot through the eye at the end. Is this a symbol of the disaster that can come from seeing too much? But note that it is the evil Cross who then tells Katherine not to look, for he desires nothing more than to cover up his past crimes so that he can commit more of them. Earlier, Jake had looked into Evelyn's eye, discovering 'a flaw in the iris… a sort of birthmark' – a clue to the fact that her own father sexually abused her. If there's no one like Jake who will look for such clues, what chance is there of ever stopping this kind of abuse? The fact that Jake may share some of Cross's violent tendencies does not make him equivalent in evil, and the fact that Jake fails to prevent Cross from continuing his predation does not invalidate such attempts, which are, after all, the only hope.

Factoid

Director Roman Polanski and writer Robert Towne argued over the film's ending, which Towne considered too bleak, calling it 'the tunnel at the end of the light'.[10] Towne had wanted Evelyn to kill Cross and then escape to Mexico with Katherine.

Taxi Driver (1976)

Directed by: Martin Scorsese
Written by: Paul Schrader
Produced by: Michael and Julia Phillips
Edited by: Tom Rolf and Melvin Shapiro
Cinematography: Michael Chapman
Cast: Robert De Niro (*Travis Bickle*), Jodie Foster (*Iris*), Cybill Shepherd (*Betsy*), Harvey Keitel (*Sport*)

Plot

Vietnam veteran Travis Bickle drives a taxi in the urban jungle of New York City, where he sees 'all the animals come out at night': whores, pimps, drunks, drug addicts and the mentally deranged. Travis idealises a blonde campaign worker named Betsy, who appears to him 'like an angel out of this filthy mess'. However, when he takes her to a porno film on their first date, she rejects him. Betsy works for presidential candidate Palantine, a man once admired by Travis for his plan to clean up the city, but now Travis seems to see Palantine as part of the problem, a false saviour and a rival for Betsy's attentions. Meanwhile, Travis also takes an interest in Iris, a preteen prostitute who works for a pimp named Sport. Travis wants to save her from a life of exploitation and return her to her parents, even though Iris tells him how bad things were back home: 'She doesn't want to be rescued, but that doesn't matter to him.'[11] Travis steels himself for his mission, exercising to make his body hard, holding his arm over a stove flame and firing guns at a practice range. Travis makes an attempt to assassinate Palantine at a campaign rally, but this fails when Travis is spotted by security guards and chased away before he can get close enough to his target to shoot. Travis then goes to the cheap hotel where Iris turns tricks. Travis shoots her pimp Sport in the stomach but is in turn shot by him in the neck. When a hulking assistant keeps coming at him, Travis shoots off three of the man's fingers, stabs him in the hand with a knife and puts a bullet through his head, spattering the wall with blood. Travis then tries to shoot himself in the head, but his gun is all out of bullets. Travis recovers. Iris's parents write him a thank-you letter for saving their daughter. The tabloids hail Travis as a hero. He goes back to driving a cab, as lonely and paranoid as ever, suggesting that it is only a matter of time before all this happens again.

Comments

When Travis wreaks bloody slaughter to 'save' Iris, she is terrified rather than grateful, as if unsure who is the bigger threat: the pimp who exploits her or this rampaging, righteous avenger. Earlier she had asked Travis, 'What makes you so high and mighty?... Didn't you ever try looking at your own eyeballs in the mirror?' At the end of the film when Travis looks in the rear-view mirror of his cab, he does a paranoid double take as though he had caught some evil stranger's eyes staring back at him – eyes that are his own. In his apartment, Travis practises for his confrontation with the villain by standing in front of the mirror. 'I'm faster than you,' he says, quick-drawing his gun on himself. 'You talkin' to *me*?' he asks, as if confused about who is challenging whom, who is the hero and who the enemy. Sport first calls Travis a 'cowboy', but when Travis shaves his hair into a Mohawk and stands looking at Sport who wears beads and a headband, it is as though 'Indian' confronts 'Indian'; there is no clear 'good guy'. Sport pimps Iris out to johns, but Travis takes Betsy to an X-rated movie: 'He really wants to get this pure white girl into that dark porno theatre,'[12] says writer Paul Schrader, 'to shove her face in the filth that he felt, to dirty her, to say, "Look at this: this is what I'm really like. How could you love someone like me?"'[13] Travis fears that he himself is the scum he has to save the city from, which is why he is so violent in his self-righteousness and why he is so ready to turn the gun on himself, to take himself out with the rest of the trash. Betsy says that Travis reminds her of a song about 'a prophet and a pusher… a walking contradiction'. Travis is sickened by the drug addicts, drunks and pimps he sees on the city streets, but he himself pops pills, pours liquor on his breakfast cereal and has a degrading view of women and sex. When Travis tries to pull himself together through military exercise and commit to 'total organisation', he becomes instead only more deranged, a hard body as aimless weapon – 'organis-ised'. Travis has lost all sense of where the evil lies. He ends up firing wildly at any target – Palantine the politician, Sport the pimp – and ultimately even at himself.

Body Heat (1981)

Directed by: Lawrence Kasdan
Written by: Lawrence Kasdan
Produced by: Fred T Gallo
Edited by: Carol Littleton
Cinematography: Richard H Kline
Cast: William Hurt (*Ned Racine*), Kathleen Turner (*Matty Walker*), Richard Crenna (*Edmund Walker*), Ted Danson (*Peter Lowenstein*), JA Preston (*Oscar Grace*), Mickey Rourke (*Teddy Lewis*)

Plot

During a Florida heat wave, lawyer Ned meets married woman Matty at a band concert. She drips cherry ice on her white dress and asks him if he wants to lick it off. Her husband Edmund is away on business, so Ned follows her home. She tempts him with the siren call of wind chimes, and he uses a chair to break through a front window, then climbs in and has sex with her on the floor. They begin an affair, alternating between rounds of steamy sex and attempts to cool off in a bathtub filled with ice cubes. They conspire to murder her husband: Ned kills him with a board in the house, then moves his body to a derelict restaurant where he makes it look as though

Edmund was accidentally killed by a falling beam during an arson gone wrong. Later, Ned is dismayed to learn that Matty forged his signature on an improper change to Edmund's will, which not only makes Ned look incompetent but also rouses police suspicions of his complicity with her. (Since the will is ruled invalid, Edmund dies intestate and she now inherits all his wealth, despite a prenuptial agreement.) Moreover, because Edmund's glasses were not found at the arson site, the police suspect that he was actually murdered in another place and his body moved. Matty calls Ned to tell him that she has located the incriminating glasses and to ask him to retrieve them from a boathouse. But Ned believes that Matty has rigged the boathouse door with a bomb, and he accuses her of this when she arrives. Matty denies it and goes to the boathouse herself, at which point an explosion occurs. Ned is imprisoned for the murders of Edmund and Matty (her body is identified from dental records). However, though the police are not persuaded, a high-school yearbook leads Ned to believe that Matty has stolen the identity of a lookalike friend and that it was this woman's body that Matty used to fake her own death in the boathouse explosion. Matty is still alive, lounging on a tropical beach and enjoying her dead husband's money.

Comments

Body Heat is sometimes referred to as retro-noir because its plot (a wife and her lover scheme to murder her husband for the money) recalls that of such classic films as *Double Indemnity* and *The Postman Always Rings Twice*. But there are some innovative aspects to Matty that make her a new kind of femme fatale. Unlike her slyly seductive counterparts in classic noir, Matty is brazenly and voraciously sexual. 'My temperature runs a couple of degrees high, around 100,' she admits, and her insatiable demands prompt Ned to say, 'You are killing me.' Matty is also outspoken about her superior intelligence, telling Ned, 'You're not too smart, are you? I like that in a man.' It's as though she's taunting him to realise that she is manipulating him, having planned all this from the beginning. (It is Matty who arranges their first meeting at the band concert, having heard that Ned is a lawyer whose incompetence she can use to her advantage.) Finally, rather than being punished for her treachery like earlier femme fatales, Matty gets away with it in the end, showing a relentlessness and achieving a success that even Ned half-admires and envies. Indeed, some viewers have found it hard not to cheer for Matty, who out-sexes and outsmarts all the men to realise her dream 'to be rich and live in an exotic land'. But even as Matty stretches out on that tropical beach, her face does not look joyful, and she virtually ignores the man lying beside her as if she has already lost interest in manipulating her next male victim. Could it be that, in acting the part of Ned's lover, she actually came to care for him? 'I fell in love with you,' she has said earlier. 'I didn't plan that.' The fact is that in the end Matty is profoundly alone, in heat and in hell on that beach, imprisoned in her own ruthlessness. Ned compares her to her gangster husband, both of them willing to do 'whatever was necessary' to satisfy their greed. But the problem for black widows is that, while well fed, they end up without any mate.

Blade Runner (1982) (Director's Cut, 1992)

Directed by: Ridley Scott
Written by: Hampton Fancher and David Peoples, from the novel *Do Androids Dream of Electric Sheep?* by Philip K Dick
Produced by: Michael Deeley
Edited by: Marsha Nakashima
Cinematography: Jordan Cronenweth
Cast: Harrison Ford (*Rick Deckard*), Rutger Hauer (*Roy Batty*), Sean Young (*Rachael*), Edward James Olmos (*Gaff*), M Emmet Walsh (*Captain Bryant*), Daryl Hannah (*Pris*), William Sanderson (*JF Sebastian*), Brion James (*Leon*), Joe Turkel (*Doctor Tyrell*), Joanna Cassidy (*Zhora*)

Plot

Los Angeles in the year 2019. In this techno-noir (combining film noir and science fiction), Deckard is a trench-coated detective and 'blade runner' who must track down and kill 'rogue replicants'. These are androids or humanoid robots that have turned against their human masters, demanding that they no longer be used as expendable warriors or as sex slaves and that they be allowed to live longer than their predetermined lifespan of four years. As Deckard follows the clues and uses his gun to 'retire' the replicants – including shooting one of the females in the back – he sees their suffering and the way they mourn for each other, and begins to wonder whether they are not more humane than he, their ruthless exterminator. Deckard begins to develop feelings for the replicants, especially one called Rachael, a femme fatale whom he 'interrogates' by giving her an empathy test which reveals that she is not human. However, Rachael turns the tables on her interrogator by asking him, 'Did you ever take that test yourself?' Rachael saves Deckard from being murdered by a replicant (Leon), even though shooting Leon means that she has killed one of her own kind. Deckard vows not to hunt Rachael, despite the fact that she has been placed on his hit list. Meanwhile, the replicant leader, 'combat model' Roy, has been doing some tracking and hunting of his own, and finally confronts Tyrell, head of the corporation that made and enslaved him. When Tyrell says he cannot extend Roy's life beyond its four-year expiration date, Roy violently unmakes his maker. Then, when Roy discovers that the female replicant he loved (Pris) has been killed by Deckard, Roy pursues and tortures him, making Deckard face his own inhumanity: 'I thought you were supposed to be good. Aren't you "the good man"?' But, just as Roy is about to take revenge on Deckard by letting him fall to his death, he pulls him to safety instead, thus displaying the kind of compassion the human Deckard should feel. Deckard then helps Rachael, the replicant with whom he has fallen in love, to escape. However, as they are leaving, he finds an origami unicorn, a sign that Deckard too may be a replicant doomed to early extinction. As Deckard and Rachael board an elevator, the door slams shut on them, as if sealing their fate. This is the way the Director's Cut of the film ends and, according to Ridley Scott, 'The elevator door was the perfect ending, but it also felt like a prison, it also felt like the end of the road. And that, I found, maybe just too oppressive for words.'[14] The theatrical version of the film adds a more hopeful coda: Deckard and Rachael make it to the green countryside, and we are told that Rachael actually has an uncertain termination date – like the rest of us.

Comments

As part of his detective work, Deckard electronically enhances a photo which contains a round mirror, allowing him to peer into it and see a female replicant (Zhora) in the bathtub. By tracing the origin of animal scales found in the actual tub, Deckard discovers that Zhora is an exotic dancer who performs with a snake. So that he can question her backstage, Deckard impersonates a decency crusader who claims to be checking her dressing room for holes, but instead of protecting her from dirty old men, Deckard seems to be one himself, sneaking furtive glances at her while she is undressed. This exploitation continues when, having determined that she is a replicant, he shoots her in the back while she is trying to escape, sending her crashing to the ground amid a bunch of female mannequins – scantily clad females like herself used as sex dolls. Standing in the wreckage, Deckard begins to detect that he himself is the voyeur and the violator from whom women need protection.

Like Zhora, Rachael initially appears to be a femme fatale with her hard, lacquered look, her cigarette and red lipstick, and her dark hair worn up in a rigid, sculpted style. When Deckard fails to find empathy by peering into her eye, she rightly suggests that he try that test on himself, for if she is a femme fatale it may be only to defend against him as a deadly man. Later, after Deckard has shown her some kindness, Rachael takes her hair down, arranging it to match the softer look of a woman in one of his family photos. This femme fatale could become a love interest if he has eyes to see her that way, and he could become something other than a killer if he would let himself be seen differently by her. At first, Deckard is violent towards Rachael, barring her exit and throwing her body backwards, but when he turns to tenderness, she responds in kind. He tells her, 'Say "kiss me"', and she says it and does, and then repeats after him, 'I want you,' herself adding, 'Put your hands on me.' If Deckard is here 'implanting' ideas in Rachael the replicant, she seems to have a few ideas of her own about what she wants him to do. Love makes them both human.

The Singing Detective (1986)

Directed by: Jon Amiel
Written by: Dennis Potter
Produced by: Kenith Trodd and John Harris
Edited by: Sue Wyatt and Bill Wright
Cinematography: Ken Westbury
Cast: Michael Gambon (*Philip E Marlow*), Janet Suzman (*Nicola*), Patrick Malahide (*Mark Binney/Finney/Raymond*), Joanne Whalley (*Nurse Mills*), Bill Paterson (*Dr Gibbon*), Jim Carter (*Mr Marlow*), Alison Steadman (*Mrs Marlow/Lili*)

Plot

The Singing Detective uses songs to link the several strands of its complicated plot. (1) Adult reality. Marlow is in a hospital ward suffering from psoriasis and arthritis – diseases that affect the skin and the joints. To escape from his pain and paralysis, he recalls scenes from (2) a mystery novel he wrote, imagining himself as the detective (like Philip Marlowe, the private-eye hero of Raymond Chandler's novels).

In this mystery set in 1940s London, Marlow is hired by Mark Binney to prove that Binney was not responsible for the death of a prostitute whose body was found in the river. However, Marlow suspects that his client, who had slept with the prostitute, may be guilty of her murder and of spying for the Nazis. While lying in his hospital bed, Marlow also has (3) a paranoid fantasy in which he imagines that his wife Nicola has been sleeping with a man named Mark Finney and that the two of them are in cahoots to steal Marlow's screenplay. Nicola seduces Marlow into signing away the rights to the screenplay, but when Finney won't give her the lead part in the film, she stabs him in the throat and then dies as a result of jumping into the river while trying to elude the police. Finally, Marlow also thinks back to (4) childhood memories, in which he falsely accused a fellow schoolboy (Mark Binney) of having befouled their teacher's desk. In addition, the child Marlow remembers witnessing Mark Binney's father having sex with Marlow's mother in the woods. The young Marlow later confronted her about this, and soon afterwards she committed suicide by throwing herself in the river. It was also at this time in his life that his terrible skin-and-joint disease first began to manifest itself, the illness that has now landed him in the hospital. In the end, the various strands of the plot come together, with the detective Marlow shooting the diseased Marlow in his sickbed. It is the detective Marlow who, cured of his illness and reunited with his wife, walks out of the hospital, and who remembers himself as a young boy thinking that when he grew up, he was going to be a detective.

Comments

At first, Marlow's mystery novel seems like an escape from reality, just as his hardboiled detective persona and cynical wisecracks protect him from feeling more pain: 'I used to think that all I wanted was the good opinion of honourable men and the ungrudging love of beautiful women. Now I know for sure that all I really want is a cigarette.' But Marlow gradually realises that he must become the true detective hero of his fiction and see through its elaborately evasive plot in order to confront the truth. Mark Finney the screenplay-stealer who slept with Marlow's wife, and Mark Binney the spy who slept with the prostitute, and Mark Binney the boy whom young Marlow accused – these are all disguises that Marlow must penetrate to get to the truth, which is his childhood memory of having watched his mother 'prostituted' by and 'stolen' from him by Mark Binney's father, who slept with her. It is this man whom Marlow blames for his mother's later suicide. And Marlow also blames his mother for having slept around, which is why she is a prostitute in his fiction and an adulterous wife in his fantasy – an unfaithful wife who rather gets what she deserves when her lover betrays her and she ends up drowned in the river. So, his mother was a femme fatale and her lover was her killer? No, Marlow is still using his detective plot to evade a deeper reality, but he can nevertheless follow the clues to find it. Marlow was hired by the fictional Mark Binney to prove that Binney did *not* do it, and when Binney himself is killed, he leaves behind a note: 'Who killed Roger Ackroyd?' *The Murder of Roger Ackroyd* is an Agatha Christie novel in which the narrator himself is guilty of the crime. Is Marlow, the narrator and author of this fiction, responsible for the death of the woman in the river? Well, what Marlow finally realises is that he has always *felt* responsible for his mother's death (since she committed suicide in the river soon after he had confronted her about her adultery) and that this secret guilt has only been fed by his blaming of others (her lover, herself) for her death. But, no, the boy Marlow should not consider himself responsible for the fact that his mother drowned herself. What this detective discovers in the end is that he was not the killer. And, since Marlow's skin-and-joint disease is a psychosomatic manifestation of his secret guilt, he is healed when this guilt goes away. The detective has cured himself by solving the mystery of his own life.

The Crying Game (1992)

Directed by: Neil Jordan
Written by: Neil Jordan
Produced by: Stephen Woolley
Edited by: Kant Pan
Cinematography: Ian Wilson
Cast: Stephen Rea (*Fergus*), Miranda Richardson (*Jude*), Jaye Davidson (*Dil*), Forest Whitaker (*Jody*)

Plot

Jody, a British soldier stationed in Ireland, is lured away from a fairground by a seductive woman named Jude so that the IRA can kidnap him and hold him hostage in return for one of their own. Fergus, assigned to guard Jody, finds himself forming a bond with his captive, and this closeness makes it hard for Fergus to shoot Jody when ordered to do so. As Fergus hesitates, Jody is run over and killed by a British armoured vehicle while trying to escape. To keep a promise made to Jody, Fergus goes to London to seek out and look after Dil, Jody's girlfriend, and gradually falls for her himself. However, as they are about to make love, Dil removes her robe to expose a flat chest and male genitals, revealing that she is a he – a gay male transvestite. While Fergus struggles to overcome his homophobic disgust at this surprise, he also has another problem to contend with: Jude and her IRA compatriots have tracked him down in order to force him to carry out a suicide mission. However, on the day of the mission, Fergus finds himself unable to go, for Dil has tied him to the bed (because she is angry with him for his role in Jody's death, but also because she wants him to love and not leave her). When Jude arrives with a gun and plans to use it on Fergus for his betrayal, Dil shoots her. Fergus then takes the rap for the murder Dil has committed, but through the years of his confinement she visits him faithfully in prison.

Comments

In some ways, Jude seems to be the stereotypical femme fatale. She seduces and entraps Jody for the IRA. She grabs Fergus's crotch and, when he rebuffs her aggressive advances, she pulls a gun from her handbag and points it at his head. Posed with her pistol on the movie poster for *The Crying Game*, Jude is the phallic woman, her femininity a mere cover for a hard cruelty. In one scene, as light streams through Venetian blinds, Jude applies make-up in front of a three-part mirror (indicating her deceptiveness). She has helmet-like hair and wears a padded-shoulder power suit. She combines masculine aggression with the spitefulness of a spurned woman, for she is insanely jealous of Fergus's relationship with Dil. Here, though, the film gives Jude's femme fatale character an extra dimension because, as the similarity in the names suggests, *Jude* is also a symbol of *Jody*'s jealousy in Fergus's mind. When Fergus moves from looking after Dil (as he had promised Jody) to loving Dil (which was not part of the promise!), the jealous Jude suddenly appears as a personification of the guilt Fergus feels for being with Jody's girlfriend. It is as though Jody returns from the grave to express his jealousy through Jude.

Dil, too, could be seen as a femme fatale. Behind her deceptively feminine allure, she is in fact a man. Fergus often sees Dil in mirrors and behind veils, but when her robe is opened, it is as though her seduction of him has led to a betrayal, for she is not the woman she had seemed to be. Yet Dil is really only a femme fatale in Fergus's mind, for it is his own homophobia that makes him fear her. Fergus claims that, before Dil's gender was revealed, he did not know that she was a man, but it's possible that Fergus did know and denied it to himself, just as it's possible that Fergus's love for Dil is an extension of his love for Jody. When Fergus is being intimate with Dil, he keeps having fantasies of Jody. Is this because a guilty Fergus feels a jealous Jody watching him with Dil, or because Fergus is actually expressing his love for Jody through Dil? Fergus even cuts

Dil's hair short like Jody's, has Dil dress in Jody's cricket whites and takes her to a hotel as if they were on a 'honeymoon'. This is all ostensibly to hide her from the IRA, but why does Fergus choose this particular disguise for Dil if not to remake her into Jody? According to actor Stephen Rea (Fergus), 'The emotional journey is that Fergus realises that you can love anyone... race, gender, nationality are all meaningless.'[15] When Dil shoots the jealous Jude, perhaps this is a sign that Fergus no longer feels guilty about his relationship with Dil, that he no longer believes Jody would be jealous of it. And when Fergus goes to prison for Dil and welcomes her faithful visits, this may be a sign that he is overcoming his homophobia and is almost ready to receive Dil's love – but not quite yet, as indicated by the prison-glass partition that still separates them.

Se7en (1995)

Directed by: David Fincher
Written by: Andrew Kevin Walker
Produced by: Arnold Kopelson and Phyllis Carlyle
Edited by: Richard Francis-Bruce
Cinematography: Darius Khondji
Cast: Brad Pitt (*David Mills*), Morgan Freeman (*William Somerset*), Kevin Spacey (*John Doe*), Gwyneth Paltrow (*Tracy Mills*)

Plot

Detective Somerset and his junior partner Mills are trying to catch a serial killer whose murders take place over 7 days and are modelled on the 7 deadly sins. An obese man (Gluttony) is found face down in a bowl of spaghetti, having been force-fed and then kicked till his stomach bursts. A high-priced lawyer (Greed), after being forced to cut off a pound of his own flesh, is bled to death. A drug dealer (Sloth) is strapped to a bed and injected with drugs for a year while he rots away. A prostitute (Lust) is raped to death by a man wearing a knife as a strap-on dildo. A beautiful woman (Pride) has her nose cut off and then takes an overdose of sleeping pills rather than live the rest of her life with such a disfigurement. Somerset and Mills follow a trail of what appear to be promising clues to the killer's identity and whereabouts, but these prove to be a dead end. Suddenly, though, the killer (Doe) walks right into the police station and turns himself in. The detectives drive Doe to a desert location where he has said he will show them the bodies of his last two victims. At 7pm on the 7th day, a delivery van arrives with a box that contains the severed head of Mills's pregnant wife. Doe (Envy) explains that he did it because he was jealous of Mills and his normal life, and Mills (Wrath), after being taunted and goaded by Doe, shoots him in the head. Mills is arrested as the sun sets on the last of Doe's crimes, his masterwork having been completed.

Comments

By the end of *Se7en*, one of the detectives (Mills) has become a victim (of Doe's manipulation) and a killer (of Doe). This detective's actions serve less to contain the criminal's evil than they do to enable him to complete his crimes. Mills sees himself as a Serpico or supercop who is fighting his polar opposite, Doe the rampaging murderer. But Somerset warns Mills that he is no 'hero' and that Doe is 'not the Devil. He's just a man.' In fact, 'John Doe' could be any man, even Mills, because all men are capable of sins like growing so angry they commit murderous acts, as Mills does. Unfortunately, because Mills sees the killer as 'other', he is not able to recognise him as the 'same' until it is too late. If Mills had been alert to the potential killer within himself, he might not have gotten so angry at Doe's goading that he shot him, thus falling into his trap.

While Mills's naïve idealism, his image of himself as a hero, leads to his downfall, Somerset runs the risk of being too world-weary, cynical and resigned. Like the killer, Somerset seems to have no hope for sinful mankind, seeing only a fallen world wherever he looks. 'How can I bring a child into a world like this?' he asks, explaining why he had convinced his girlfriend to abort their child – and we note that Doe violently aborts a child when he kills Mills's pregnant wife. Both Somerset and Doe are alone, with no family to love or to love them back in a way that might mitigate their hopelessness. Evil seems so prevalent that Somerset can barely bring himself to fight it anymore. 'I can't get involved in this,' he says about the serial killer case, and he wants only to resign and leave this city of pervasive sin and perpetual rain. In the end, failing to stop Mills from being goaded into shooting Doe, Somerset looks heavenward – as if in a last, desperate search for God – and then drops his head in despair. However, perhaps because his friendship with Mills has made him realise that he *does* still care, Somerset decides to stay on as a detective and keep fighting for this world.

Factoid

Concerned that an overly bleak conclusion would make for bad box office, the studio pushed for some happier endings: Mills's wife could be rescued in the nick of time. The decapitated head in the box could belong to one of Mills's dogs, not his wife. Somerset could be the one to shoot Doe, and that way Mills would not be arrested and could still have his whole life ahead of him.

The Usual Suspects (1995)

Directed by: Bryan Singer
Written by: Christopher McQuarrie
Produced by: Bryan Singer and Michael McDonnell
Edited by: John Ottman
Cinematography: Newton Thomas Sigel
Cast: Gabriel Byrne (*Dean Keaton*), Stephen Baldwin (*Michael McManus*), Chazz Palminteri (*Dave Kujan*), Kevin Spacey (*Roger 'Verbal' Kint*), Pete Postlethwaite (*Kobayashi*)

Plot

A cargo ship explodes, leaving 27 burned bodies. Customs agent Kujan interrogates Verbal Kint, the one surviving member of a gang of thieves who first met each other six weeks ago when they were pulled in for a police line-up. Keaton, a crooked ex-cop, had been trying to go straight but kept being hounded by police for his past crimes. In the jail's holding cell, Keaton, Verbal and three other men form a gang and decide to rob some corrupt cops who are providing an illegal 'taxi service' for a diamond smuggler. The heist succeeds, and the gang take the diamonds to a fence, who puts them on to another job, robbing a jeweller (Berg). This time, though, there is bloodshed: Verbal shoots Berg when the man pulls a gun, and inside the man's briefcase they find drugs. A lawyer (Kobayashi) explains that his boss, legendary criminal mastermind Keyser Soze, was the one behind the job and was glad to have Berg dead. In fact, Soze had been behind everything, even pulling strings to have the men brought in for that police line-up because, unbeknownst to them, their past thieving had trespassed on his criminal turf and so he was now punishing them and using them for his own ends. Kobayashi tells them that Soze will have their families killed unless the gang agree to raid a cargo ship and destroy the drugs on board. The gang shoot the ship's guards but find no drugs and are themselves picked off one by one by Soze himself, who had merely used them to clear the way so that he could board the ship, kill another one of his enemies (Marquez) and then blow everything up. At least this is Verbal's version of events, but agent Kujan thinks that the story is a fabrication to allow Keaton – the real Soze – to fake his death and evade capture. However, after Verbal has left the police station, Kujan realises that Verbal has constructed his tale based on objects and bulletin-board notices he saw in the office where he was interrogated, including the word 'Kobayashi' on the bottom of Kujan's coffee mug. Verbal is Soze! It is the criminal himself, a very unreliable narrator, who told this tale in order to *prevent* his own detection.

Comments

Verbal seems to have a withered arm with which he is unable to flick a flip-top lighter to light his cigarette – or to set fire to the ship. However, his disability is only an act, for Verbal is really quite adept at lighting things up and destroying lives. But what makes other people's fuses so easily lit, sending them to hell? Verbal is a devil who succeeds in tempting people to give way to their own worst natures, particularly their desire for revenge. Keaton is a crooked cop trying to go straight, but Verbal, who believes that 'a man can't change who he is', convinces Keaton that the police will always consider him a criminal so he might as well remain one, commit a robbery and strike back at them (stealing the diamonds from the smuggler exposes the corrupt cops and their illegal 'taxi service'). Verbal (aka Soze) tempts Keaton into becoming like himself, a confirmed criminal who lives only for revenge. There is the suggestion that Soze once had the potential to be a different kind of man, but when enemies took his wife and children hostage, he decided to demonstrate his invulnerability by killing his own family, which ironically 'destroys him. His family was all he had, and now he is this utterly ruthless shell of a man.'[16] Soze goes on to kill all his enemies' families, thereby creating the myth of himself as inveterately evil and vengeful. Verbal/Soze also manipulates agent Kujan by playing on that man's desire for revenge against Keaton. By seeming to defend Keaton, Verbal cleverly arouses Kujan's suspicions, leading him to the false conclusion that Keaton is Soze. In fact, Verbal seems to bring out the bad behaviour in most of the film's male characters, turning them into disciples of his devilish self: *K*eaton, *K*ujan and *K*obayashi are all mini-versions of Verbal *K*int/*K*eyser Soze.

L.A. Confidential (1997)

Directed by: Curtis Hanson
Written by: Brian Helgeland and Curtis Hanson, from the novel by James Ellroy

Produced by: Arnon Milchan, Curtis Hanson and Michael Nathanson
Edited by: Peter Honess
Cinematography: Dante Spinotti
Cast: Kevin Spacey (*Jack Vincennes*), Russell Crowe (*Bud White*), Guy Pearce (*Edmund 'Ed' Exley*), James Cromwell (*Capt Dudley Smith*), David Strathairn (*Pierce Patchett*), Kim Basinger (*Lynn Bracken*), Danny DeVito (*Sid Hudgens*)

Plot

1950s Los Angeles. Ed, Bud and Jack are three LAPD detectives who, though initially at odds with one another, eventually work together to solve the case of a mass murder at the Nite Owl coffee shop. At first Ed suspects three junkies, but they turn out to be guilty of kidnapping and rape, not of the Nite Owl homicides. Bud discovers that one of the Nite Owl victims was a surgically altered call girl working for a man named Patchett: 'Patchett's running whores cut to look like movie stars. This is how their dreams of Hollywood turned out.' Patchett has also been blackmailing the whores' clients by having tabloid journalist Sid snap pictures of them in compromising positions. Jack inadvertently finds this out when his own deal with Sid – busting celebrities for minor offences and tipping Sid off so that he is there to take photos – turns out to involve Jack in the death of a young male prostitute, who was killed to gain political leverage over a gay DA. Jack informs his police captain (Dudley) about the blackmail scheme, and Dudley shoots Jack dead. Dudley turns out to have been in cahoots with Patchett – and to be the one behind the Nite Owl murders, which were committed for control of LA's drugs racket. 'How can organised crime exist in the city with the best police force in the world?' It can when the police captain is head of the criminal organisation! In order to block the investigation and remain undiscovered, Dudley now turns his detectives against each other by having Bud discover photos of Ed having sex with Lynn, the call girl whom Bud loves. But, after a brutal fight, the two detectives realise that Dudley is trying to distract them and they team up. In the finale, just as Dudley is about to shoot Ed, Bud stabs Dudley in the leg. Dudley then shoots Bud, but Ed has had the time to pick up a shotgun and gain the upper hand, getting Dudley to drop his weapon. Realising that he will never be able to prove the case against Dudley in court, Ed shoots him dead.

Comments

Justly famous for the twists and turns of its investigative plot (the case is so complicated it often pushes the bounds of viewer comprehension), *L.A. Confidential* also deserves praise for the complexity of its detective characters. Jack is the technical adviser to a TV cop show, *Badge of Honor*. He's so proud of being a 'celebrity cop' that he doesn't realise how dishonourable he has really become, taking money from sleazy Sid to set up busts for the tabloid press. But when a male prostitute dies during one of these set-ups, Jack not only feels responsible (as he indirectly is) but also sees that he too has been a whore, in effect selling his badge for payoffs and photo publicity. This shock of recognition induces Jack to reform and become a true cop, so it is only fitting that, after Jack is killed for investigating the blackmail scheme, an episode of *Badge of Honor* is dedicated to him.

When Bud was young, he witnessed his father beat his mother to death. Ever since then, Bud has been driven to avenge himself on abusive men – so driven that the corrupt captain Dudley is able to use Bud's brutality as 'muscle' against Dudley's enemies, including rival criminals and good cops like Ed. When Bud finds the photo of Ed having sex with Lynn, Bud attacks not only Ed but Lynn as well, beating the woman he loves and has vowed to protect. This moment, which shocks Bud into realising that he has become a woman-beater like his father, also frees Bud from the compulsion to be the perfect opposite of his father. Now able to think for himself, Bud can become a real investigator and follow the clues to the true culprit and the proper object of Bud's rage: Dudley.

As for Ed, he is so self-righteous that he doesn't see how much of his 'by the book' mentality is really a cover for his own career ambitions, as when he disapproves of his fellow cops' wrongdoing and receives a promotion for testifying against them. Even worse, Ed's too-tightly-held belief in his own goodness and rightness makes him easy to manipulate, and Dudley uses Ed to get minor crooks to confess and to get slightly 'bent' cops out of the way so that the wholly corrupt Dudley and his handpicked criminals can rule the city. But Ed finally recognises that he can be wrong (about the three junkies being the Nite Owl killers, about Bud being a mere brute, about the pure goodness of his own motives), and that is when he is able to detect the corruption behind Dudley's 'good cop' act and to bring it to an end.

The Matrix (1999)

Directed by: The Wachowski Brothers (Andy and Larry Wachowski)
Written by: The Wachowski Brothers
Produced by: Joel Silver
Edited by: Zach Staenberg
Cinematography: Bill Pope
Cast: Keanu Reeves (*Neo*), Laurence Fishburne (*Morpheus*), Carrie-Anne Moss (*Trinity*), Hugo Weaving (*Agent Smith*), Joe Pantoliano (*Cypher*)

Plot

Neo lives a double life. By day he is a software programmer, a lowly worker slaving away in his cubicle. By night he is a computer hacker, secretly rebelling against his corporate masters. Following a series of clues beginning with a mysterious message on his computer, Neo discovers the existence of an armed underground resistance to corporate power. Rebel leader Morpheus gives Neo the choice between taking a blue pill whereby his life will go blindly on as usual, and taking a red pill where he will see a terrible truth. Neo takes the red pill and finds out that the real world he thought he was living in is in fact a software program: 'You've been living in a dream world, Neo... The Matrix is a computer-generated dream world built to keep us under control.' The entire city that Neo and his co-workers inhabit is a digital simulation designed to pacify their minds and cover up the truth: in reality, their comatose bodies are being used as human batteries to power intelligent machines that now rule the world. Morpheus believes that Neo is 'The One', the prophesied messiah who will successfully hack the Matrix, destroy the illusory power of its code and free the people from its enslavement. When one member of the resistance (Cypher) turns traitor and allows Morpheus to be captured by the agents who work for the machines, Neo must jack in to the Matrix and use his mind to bend and break the rules, including stopping the agents' bullets in midair, in order to save Morpheus. In the end, Neo sends an unauthorised message to every worker's computer, trying to get us all to wake up and fight back against corporate control over our lives.

Comments

One nasty surprise for this Neo-noir detective is that his epistemological query has ontological consequences. When Neo follows the clues to the meaning of the Matrix, he discovers that the bottom drops out of his world: 'reality' is a hoax; it really was all a dream. The end of his active pursuit of truth is to find out that he is in fact totally passive, his mind programmed by machines, his body suspended in a vat and being drained of its life energy. However, contained within this vision of seeming hopelessness there is a further revelation which changes everything: Neo is 'The One'. (The word *one* is hidden as an anagram within *neo*.) Rather than being a passive sufferer, he will be the agent of everyone's salvation, freeing us from our worker-drone enslavement to corporate machines. Neo's impotence is actually omnipotence. The world is a dream, but we can awaken from it to a better reality, if we have the courage to rebel. Early in the film, we see that Neo keeps his pirated software disks inside a hollowed-out book, *Simulacra and Simulation* by Jean Baudrillard. Here we have a metaphor for the hidden reality behind the simulation, but also for the courage of the hacker who intervenes to challenge the film's evil corporate system. Interestingly, all the machines' agents look alike with their suits and slicked-back hair – and they all look like Neo's company boss, who wants Neo to look and act just like him: 'You have a problem with authority... You believe that you're special, that somehow the rules do not apply to you.' That's right: Neo is a champion of individuality against corporate conformity. He wants to speak his mind (and not have his mouth glued shut). He wants the freedom to move about and associate with other individuals (and not have his movements tracked by a bug or be used as a means to locate his friends for elimination). By contrast, Cypher wants to forget harsh reality and be returned to the dream, where steaks tasted good because he believed the advertising that told him they did, and where women satisfied him because he believed that pornographic pin-ups (like the Woman in Red) were all that he desired. In reality, Cypher finds that female rebel Trinity doesn't respond to him (because he treats her like a pin-up) and that food can taste bad (since he is using his actual tongue to taste it). What Cypher wants is a narcissistic corporate cocoon so that he doesn't have to deal with any resistant reality. Neo, on the other hand, recognises Trinity as a person, not a pin-up, and in response she chooses to kiss him. Each tastes the reality of the other's lips as they touch, bringing their minds back to being grounded in their bodies.

Sin City (2005)

Directed by: Frank Miller and Robert Rodriguez, based on the graphic novels by Frank Miller
Produced by: Elizabeth Avellán, Frank Miller and Robert Rodriguez
Edited by: Robert Rodriguez
Cinematography: Robert Rodriguez

Cast: Bruce Willis (*Hartigan*), Nick Stahl (*Roark Jr/Yellow Bastard*), Jessica Alba (*Nancy*), Mickey Rourke (*Marv*), Jaime King (*Goldie/Wendy*), Elijah Wood (*Kevin*), Rutger Hauer (*Cardinal Roark*), Clive Owen (*Dwight*), Rosario Dawson (*Gail*), Benicio Del Toro (*Jackie Boy*), Brittany Murphy (*Shellie*)

Plot

Veteran cop Hartigan saves 11-year-old Nancy from Roark Jr, a paedophile whom Hartigan shoots in the groin. Years later, after being wrongly imprisoned for the paedophile's crimes, Hartigan finds Nancy again, in a strip bar where she has become an exotic dancer. However, Roark Jr – now a yellow mutant as a result of chemical treatments to restore his manhood – has trailed Hartigan to the bar in order to prey on Nancy again. Hartigan defeats the villain, ripping out his new genitals. Elsewhere in Sin City, an ugly mug named Marv enjoys a night of lovemaking with Goldie, a hooker with a heart of gold, only to find her dead in bed the next morning and himself framed for her murder. After some detective work, Marv discovers that Goldie is one of a series of prostitutes killed by a cannibal (Kevin) and a corrupt priest (Cardinal Roark). Marv takes revenge on them both, making sure that the cannibal is devoured by his own wolf-dog. In another storyline, a fugitive (Dwight) protects his girlfriend (Shellie) from her abusive ex-boyfriend (Jackie Boy) by threatening to castrate him with a razor. When Jackie Boy tries to take out his rage on other women by getting sexually aggressive with them, a sword-wielding prostitute (Miho) chops off his hand and slits his throat. Men seeking retribution then kidnap Dwight's former lover Gail, but he arranges to exchange Jackie Boy's severed head for her safe return, while also leading the men into a trap where they are vanquished by the women.

Comments

Sin City has been criticised for having one-dimensional characters and a simplistic opposition between good and evil – a 'moral polarisation' that is 'not really reflective of the ambivalence of film noir'.[17] However, writer and co-director Frank Miller has said that the 'spooky' black-and-white 'look' of his noir graphics, all those 'shadows and blinds', are 'metaphors for the torment, or the rage, or the self-hatred, or the despair the characters are going through'.[18] Miller's heroes are complex, internally conflicted characters, and in *Sin City* they confront their own confusion in order to achieve 'a fierce moral clarity in which each person makes his moral decisions'.[19] The film's prologue may set the pattern: a man tells a woman that he will save her from whatever she is scared of and then, as he holds her in his arms, shoots her dead. Like this man, Hartigan too has a dark side, an aspect of his character that makes him potentially more villain than hero. After saving Nancy from the paedophile, Hartigan himself is tempted by this woman much younger than he. It is odd that Hartigan is imprisoned for the paedophile's abduction of the child Nancy, and also strange that Hartigan leads the paedophile to the teenage Nancy. Hartigan, despite being acutely aware of their age difference, must take a cold shower so as not to give way to his urge to sleep with her – and this is exactly when the sickly yellow paedophile attacks him, as if Hartigan were being assailed by his own worst impulses, which he must decisively defeat if he is to be the hero.

And consider Marv, who has the face of an ugly brute: his 'angel' Goldie ends up as dead meat after a night in his arms, and he subsequently finds out she was a whore. Goldie 'comes back' in the form of her identical twin sister Wendy to accuse Marv of the murder, as if he were haunted by the thought that he might indeed have done it. Marv's adversaries are a cannibal, who reduces women to meat, and a corrupt priest, who frequents prostitutes but believes they deserve to be punished. As Cardinal Roark says, Kevin 'ate their souls, and I joined in. They were all whores.' By defeating these evil men, Marv conquers his own misogynistic impulses and proves himself able to see women as being both sexual *and* spiritual. 'She smells like angels ought to smell,' Marv thinks of Goldie, and he says it doesn't matter to him if she was a prostitute. Marv is rewarded when twin Wendy gives herself to him, as if his love for Goldie had brought her back from the grave to be reunited with him.

As for Dwight, Jackie Boy would seem to be his dark double. Shellie says that she only dated Jackie Boy (her old, abusive boyfriend) before Dwight showed up with his new face (the result of plastic surgery). It's as though Dwight is a reconstructed (more woman-friendly) version of Jackie Boy, but could Dwight slip back into his old ways? Shellie apologises for having 'done some dumb things' like dating Jackie Boy, but Dwight says that he understands since he himself is 'one of those dumb things'. He knows what he was and could still be again if he doesn't fight his own abusive tendencies springing from male insecurity. So Dwight sides with the women when they cut macho Jackie Boy down to size. (The hand-chopping and throat-slitting are symbolic castrations.) And Dwight joins with his ex-girlfriend Gail in the fight against misogynistic men, working to conquer his own fears of strong female sexuality: 'My warrior woman,' he thinks of Gail as she kisses him. 'She almost yanks my head clean off, shoving my mouth into hers so hard it hurts.' Rather than trying to dominate and possess Gail, Dwight realises that the woman he loves will always belong to herself as much as she belongs to him: 'You'll always be mine – always, and never.'

Watchmen (2009)

Directed by: Zack Snyder
Written by: David Hayter and Alex Tse, from the graphic novel by Alan Moore and Dave Gibbons
Produced by: Lawrence Gordon, Lloyd Levin and Deborah Snyder
Edited by: William Hoy
Cinematography: Larry Fong
Cast: Malin Akerman (*Laurie Jupiter/Silk Spectre II*), Billy Crudup (*Dr Manhattan/Jon Osterman*), Matthew Goode (*Adrian Veidt/Ozymandias*), Carla

Gugino (*Sally Jupiter/Silk Spectre*), Jackie Earle Haley (*Walter Kovacs/ Rorschach*), Jeffrey Dean Morgan (*Edward Blake/The Comedian*), Patrick Wilson (*Dan Dreiberg/Nite Owl II*)

Plot

It is 1985 in an alternate universe where, because of superheroes, America won the Vietnam War; Watergate reporters Woodward and Bernstein have been assassinated; and Nixon has just been elected to a fifth term as President. Walking the mean streets of a crime-ridden city, Rorschach wears a trench coat, a fedora hat and a white mask with an ever-changing inkblot pattern. When a man in a high-rise apartment is murdered by a mysterious assailant, Rorschach investigates and comes to believe that someone is killing off former superheroes so that they will not be able to stop an impending nuclear war. The murder victim (the Comedian) and Rorschach were once members of a league of costumed crime-fighters known as the Watchmen, until a law banning 'masked vigilantes' forced most of them into retirement. Following the clues, Rorschach retraces the Comedian's path on his last days to the apartment of another superhero (Moloch), but this turns out to be a trap laid by the killer to get Rorschach arrested for Moloch's murder. However, Rorschach's friends Dan and Laurie don their costumes again and break Rorschach out of prison. Rorschach's detective work reveals that 'the smartest man on the planet', Ozymandias, has tricked 'the country's most powerful weapon', Dr Manhattan, into building a doomsday device. Rorschach and Dan rush to Ozymandias's Antarctic hideaway to prevent him from detonating the device, but unlike your classic comic-book superheroes, they are too late. Ozymandias's nuclear bombs kill millions, but he explains that he has done it to save billions. The Americans and the Soviets had been headed towards total nuclear annihilation, but now, as long as they believe that Dr Manhattan was responsible for the blasts, they will be united in peace against him as their common enemy.

Rorschach is the only one who refuses to go along with this lie, but before he can tell the world the truth, Dr Manhattan vaporises him to ensure his silence. However, Rorschach has sent the journals detailing his investigation to a newspaper office where a young assistant is looking for a provocative story to publish...

Comments

As Rorschach narrates the journal record of his investigation in hardboiled voiceover, he is 'constantly commenting on society, on the other characters, and on the mystery that's unfolding', director Zack Snyder says. 'Rorschach is this uncompromising, unrelenting seeker of justice in a noirish, throwback style.'[20] Indeed, some see Rorschach as retrograde in the extreme, a right-wing vigilante who reduces everything to good versus evil – a contrast as stark as that between the black and white on his mask. Rorschach can also seem callous and nihilistic. He says that after taking a meat cleaver to the head of a child molester who had used it to chop up a female victim, 'Whatever was left of Walter Kovacs [Rorschach's real name] died that night with that little girl.' According to Jackie Earle Haley (the former child actor who plays Rorschach), 'I think every bit of vigilante work he does is protecting that inner child. With every cleaver strike... he's protecting the child that he was.'[21] Rorschach now considers the mask he wears to be his only face, and he puts it on as a kind of armour to make him 'free from fear or weakness'. (When the police arrest and unmask him, he shouts, 'Give me back my face!') In hardening himself against evil, Rorschach sometimes seems to have lost all humanity and hope. Like *Taxi Driver*'s Travis Bickle (on whom his character is partly based), Rorschach thinks of the city as a cesspool and of its citizens as vermin. (It's no accident that one of his disguises is as a prophet of doom who carries a sign warning that 'THE END IS NIGH'.)

And yet, if Rorschach had really given up on humanity, would he continue to hunt evil? Don't his actions imply some remnant of faith that goodness might one day prevail? Rorschach is the only member of the Watchmen who refused to hang up his costume despite the ban on superheroes, and his tenacious opposition to crime inspires Dan and Laurie to begin fighting again. Rorschach's capacity for fellow feeling is shown by the fact that he seeks out his former colleagues to warn them that their kind are being killed. Indeed, Rorschach's search for the killer seems to be motivated as much by a desire to renew old friendships as it is to punish the wrongdoer. Rorschach's feelings are actually visible through his mask, as its ever-changing inkblots convey his facial expressions. At the end, Rorschach takes off his mask, revealing his vulnerability as he accuses the godlike Dr Manhattan of not having cared enough about humanity to prevent Ozymandias's nuclear blasts. Knowing that Dr Manhattan is going to kill him, Rorschach calls out for him to do it now as tears fall from his agonised face. Some will see the nihilistic Rorschach as simply desiring to die. Some will see his simplistic worldview as obsolete. (It is Ozymandias who set off the blasts, and Rorschach believes the world should be told this and Ozymandias should be punished, even if this means an end to the peace.) But others will see that it is Rorschach who has faith that people can still make peace even if they know the truth. It is Rorschach who realises that, in going along with Ozymandias's lie, the other superheroes are complicit in the mass murder by nuclear blast that he has committed. It is the hardboiled hero, Rorschach, who in the end cries for humanity.

NEO-NOIR AUTEURS

THE COEN BROTHERS

Blood Simple (1984)

Directed by: Joel Coen
Written by: Joel and Ethan Coen
Produced by: Ethan Coen
Edited by: Roderick Jaynes (Joel and Ethan Coen) and Don Wiegmann
Cinematography: Barry Sonnenfeld
Cast: John Getz (*Ray*), Frances McDormand (*Abby*), Dan Hedaya (*Julian Marty*), M Emmet Walsh (*Loren Visser*)

Plot

A desert town in Texas. Bartender Ray sleeps with Abby, the wife of Marty, owner of a bar and strip club. After Marty is shown compromising photos of the couple in bed together, he attempts to rape Abby in revenge, but she breaks his finger and kicks him in the groin. Marty then hires Visser, a sleazy private eye, to kill the illicit lovers. When Visser presents Marty with a photo of the couple's bullet-ridden bodies, Marty pays him for the murder, but not before secretly locking the photo in his safe in case he needs to use it later against Visser. Visser is equally mistrustful of Marty and shoots him, using a gun the private eye had stolen from Abby's purse. Later, Ray shows up at the bar. (It turns out that Visser had merely doctored the photo of Ray and Abby to make it look as though they were murdered.) When Ray sees Marty's body and Abby's gun, he believes that Abby has shot Marty, and so Ray attempts to cover up the crime to protect the woman he loves. But, after Ray has driven the body to a crop field in order to bury it at night, he discovers that Marty is not yet dead. Marty attempts to shoot Ray with Abby's gun, but Ray disarms Marty and buries him alive. Ray returns to Abby, but miscommunication feeds a growing mistrust between them. Abby, who doesn't know that Marty is dead, can't figure out why Ray won't tell her what is going on unless Ray himself is plotting against her, and Ray, who thinks that Abby shot Marty, can't understand why she won't admit it – unless she is planning to pin that crime on Ray. Meanwhile, Visser has realised that he left the incriminating photo behind at the crime scene, along with an engraved cigarette lighter, and he fears that Ray and Abby will use these against him. As Ray and Abby are talking in her apartment, he warns her to turn out the lights, but she is more afraid of Ray himself than of anyone who may be watching them from outside the window. As a consequence, Visser is able to shoot Ray dead with a long-distance rifle. Visser then goes after Abby inside the apartment. He reaches his arm out the bathroom window and around to the one in the adjoining room in an attempt to catch her, but she uses a knife to pin his hand to the windowsill. Visser then fills the wall dividing him and her with bullet holes, causing shafts of light to shoot in her direction. He works his hand free and intends to finish her off, but she recovers her own gun and, firing through the door that separates their rooms, shoots him dead.

Comments

The title *Blood Simple* is taken from Dashiell Hammett's noir novel, *Red Harvest*, in which the narrator muses that 'This damned burg's getting me. If I don't get away soon I'll be going blood-simple like the natives... Play with murder enough and it gets you one of two ways.

It makes you sick, or you get to like it.'[22] Along with murder we could add adultery: both tend to make the characters go crazy. From the moment Abby is unfaithful to Marty, her guilt feeds her fear that he will be coming to take revenge. Marty – in the form of his private eye or his German shepherd – seems to be watching Abby in bed with Ray. Marty appears to her in a nightmare, saying that Ray plans to kill her, and Abby sees Ray sitting with his cowboy boots on a table, just as Marty used to do, as if Marty were coming to get her in the form of Ray. Abby mistakes a phone call with no voice on the other line as coming from Marty (it is Visser who called), just as she mistakes her attacker at the end for Marty (when it is really Visser). Abby's guilt over the adultery leads to a paranoid fear that *everyone* is Marty and that *everyone* is trying to kill her.

In a similar fashion, Ray, who first mortifies Marty by sleeping with his wife before actually burying him alive, cannot cleanse himself of Marty's blood. The nylon jacket Ray uses to wipe up Marty's blood from the floor only seems to spread it around; Marty's body revives to cough blood over Ray; and red stains seep through the towel used to cover up Marty's blood on Ray's car seat. 'He was alive when I buried him,' Ray confesses to Abby, just as a newspaper hits the front door with a bang like a gunshot, and later Ray is shot dead in the back by an assailant unknown to him, as if killed by his own paranoid fear over what he did to Marty (though the actual shooter is Visser).

Finally, there is Visser himself. If murder makes Ray 'sick', then Visser's problem is that he has gotten 'to like it'. Yes, Visser shoots Marty because he doesn't trust him, but he also seems to enjoy the killing. Yet if one is attracted to murder, then one is in a sense driven to kill again and again – a compulsion which eventually leads Visser to his own demise. And Visser seems as vulnerable as everyone else to fear. He keeps on killing in an attempt to get back the incriminating photo and lighter, but Visser's desperation is pure paranoia: Marty and Abby aren't planning to use the lighter against him; they don't even know who he is!

Fargo (1996)

Directed by: Joel Coen
Written by: Joel and Ethan Coen
Produced by: Ethan Coen
Edited by: Roderick Jaynes (Joel and Ethan Coen)
Cinematography: Roger Deakins
Cast: Frances McDormand (*Marge Gunderson*), William H Macy (*Jerry Lundegaard*), Steve Buscemi (*Carl Showalter*), Peter Stormare (*Gaear Grimsrud*), Harve Presnell (*Wade Gustafson*)

Plot

Bleak, snow-covered North Dakota and Minnesota. Car salesman Jerry has his own wife kidnapped so that his father-in-law (Wade) will pay the ransom, which Jerry plans to split between himself and the kidnappers (Carl and Gaear). At one point, Jerry tries to call the kidnapping off when it seems that Wade is willing to lend him funds so that he can invest in a parking lot, but it turns out that his greedy father-in-law just wants to make money off the investment for himself. The criminals abduct Jerry's wife but end up shooting a nosy state trooper and two onlookers who were just driving by. The swaggering Wade insists on delivering the ransom money himself and tries to shoot it out with Carl, who kills him and buries part of the money. Returning to his partner-in-crime, Carl finds that Gaear has indifferently killed their hostage, Jerry's wife, for whimpering too loudly. Carl and Gaear then become embroiled in a ridiculous quarrel, with Gaear insisting that they 'split' the getaway car as well as the money. Gaear eventually takes an axe to Carl. In counterpoint to the actions of these bumbling criminals, police chief Marge Gunderson conducts a savvy investigation, despite the fact that she is heavily pregnant. Step by step Marge follows the clues which take her from analysing the first roadside crime scene (the kidnappers' licence plates are from Jerry's car dealership), to questioning a car mechanic (one of Jerry's co-workers, who first put him in touch with the kidnappers), and on to interrogating Jerry himself, who flees the interview when things get too hot for him. Marge's investigation finally leads her to the kidnappers' hideaway, where she arrives just as Gaear is disposing of Carl's body by stuffing it into a woodchipper. Marge shoots Gaear in the leg as he is fleeing, arrests him and drives him back to justice in her police car. Soon after, the police enter a motel room to apprehend Jerry, who screams and struggles as he is arrested.

Comments

Rather than taking place in a dark urban environment like the typical film noir, *Fargo* is a *film blanc* set in the white, flat expanses of the snowy Midwest. And yet such surroundings are equally oppressive in their own way. As writer/director Joel Coen has said, 'We were trying to reflect the bleak aspect of living in that area in the wintertime – what the light and this sort of landscape does psychologically.'[23] An extreme high-angle shot of Jerry scraping the ice off his car windshield in a snow-covered parking lot conveys his lonely desolation. Exposed as they are to the harsh wintry elements, these characters have nothing but each other, but Jerry has just found out that his father-in-law won't give him the loan he needs, for family feeling seems to mean nothing to this harsh patriarch. Similarly, Carl goes half-crazy from loneliness, crushed by the silence of his uncommunicative partner Gaear as the two of them sit waiting in their hideout by a frozen lake. The nearest they come to comradeship is when they have sex with two prostitutes in the same motel room and then watch TV afterwards. By contrast, Marge and her husband Norm, who also watch TV from bed, are a true married couple. Their relationship is based on love, not money, and they are constantly communicating, lending each other support to shore themselves up against a hostile environment.

The cheerful, polite and pregnant Marge is a long way from the cynical hardboiled detective of conventional film noir. Some have argued that the only way Marge can stay so chipper in a world where men are fed into woodchippers is by simply refusing to recognise that life has a dark side. So, when Marge says 'I just don't understand it' about the terrible things Gaear and others have done, some see her as declining to look any deeper into the human heart, including her own. For Marge, one critic writes, 'virtue is a kind of ignorance'.[24] However, actress Frances McDormand believes that Marge may be 'simple and on-the-surface, but she's not naïve, and she's not innocent, because she's good at her job, which gives her contact with crime and murder'.[25] First, Marge's folksiness is in part a clever interrogation tactic, as when she uses her pregnancy weight as an excuse to sit down in front of Jerry and continue questioning him. Second, Marge herself knows what it is like to be tempted, for she goes to a hotel bar to meet a former friend (Mike) to whom she is still attracted. When she finds out that Mike has lied to her (about his family situation, in order to get what he wants), she seems to realise that Jerry may have done the same and this leads her to interrogate him again. Finally, the compassion that Marge shows to the men around her (Mike, her deputy Lou, her husband Norm) reveals that at some level she does understand what makes a murderer – and what keeps a man from becoming one. If Jerry, Carl and Gaear had had someone like Marge to help them with their losses, their mistakes and their failures, it might be possible for them to see, as Marge does, 'a beautiful day' – even in the coldest, bleakest surroundings.

The Man Who Wasn't There (2001)

Directed by: Joel Coen
Written by: Joel and Ethan Coen
Produced by: Ethan Coen

Edited by: Roderick Jaynes (Joel and Ethan Coen) and Tricia Cooke
Cinematography: Roger Deakins
Cast: Billy Bob Thornton (*Ed Crane*), Frances McDormand (*Doris Crane*), James Gandolfini (*'Big Dave' Brewster*), Michael Badalucco (*Frank*), Jon Polito (*Creighton Tolliver*), Tony Shalhoub (*Freddie Riedenschneider*), Scarlett Johansson (*'Birdy' Abundas*)

Plot

Ed Crane is a small-town California barber in 1949. His wife Doris works as an accountant for department store owner 'Big Dave'. Doris and Dave are having an affair and embezzling funds to pay for a new store annex, which she would run. When a man named Tolliver offers Ed the chance to invest in a dry-cleaning business if he can get the money, Ed sends an anonymous blackmail note to Dave, threatening to expose his malfeasance unless he pays up. Ed picks up the money and takes it to Tolliver, who promptly absconds with it – but not before Dave puts two and two together, beats up Tolliver and finds out that Ed is behind the blackmail. Dave confronts Ed, attempting to strangle him, but Ed stabs Dave to death. The police arrest Doris for the killing, since she was cooking the books. An eager-to-win defence attorney takes her case, but Doris hangs herself before the trial. (Doris's ambitions to start a new career and family with Dave – she is pregnant with his child – have been dashed by his death and, as a final blow, she finds out that his claims of having been a war hero were hollow.) Ed's own hopes for a new start turn to Birdy, a teenage girl he believes could have a career as a professional pianist. But a master teacher dashes Ed's hopes by telling him that Birdy will never make a great pianist, and when Birdy attempts to console him by giving him oral sex on the drive home, Ed crashes the car. Birdy is fine, but Ed is arrested for the murder of Tolliver who, though most probably killed by Dave, was found with Ed's investment papers on his body. Ed is sentenced to the electric chair.

Comments

Despite the noirish time period, the black-and-white cinematography and the 'modern dread' and 'paranoia' pervading this film, 'the main character' in *The Man Who Wasn't There* 'couldn't be further from your conventional film noir hero, in terms of his obsessions and personality',[26] as Joel Coen has said. Rather than murdering for lust and money (like the hero in *The Postman Always Rings Twice*), Ed Crane seems passive and recessive, the affectless victim of others' actions – or of fate. But I would argue that Ed has the same desires and ambitions as everyone else. He just won't admit to them because that would mean having to take responsibility for them. Ed spends much of the movie nodding, as if he merely accepts everything that happens to him with a quiet resignation. His wife Doris's affair and Dave's success as a businessman and 'war hero' don't seem to bother Ed, who seems content to cut hair, to be 'the barber'. Yet Ed is actually so desperate to move up in the world that he believes Tolliver's lies about an investment opportunity (just as Doris fell for Dave's lies about his war record and about the opportunity for career advancement through sex and embezzlement with him). It is no coincidence that Ed's plan to get the investment money involves blackmailing Dave, for in doing so Ed is actually acting out of envy and jealousy, ruining Dave's and Doris's 'business affairs'. And when Dave attacks him for the blackmail, of course Ed must defend himself, stabbing Dave with a knife that was supposedly one of Dave's war trophies and thus puncturing Dave's 'war hero' pretensions. After the killing, Ed looks down at his hands and they are clean, for Ed has no blood on his conscience since he denies any responsibility for Dave's death. Interestingly, a scene deleted from the movie has Ed fleeing from two detectives who ask him questions, which was to be followed by another (deleted) scene in which Ed stuffs towels under a door to keep out tiny aliens who have come to get him. It would seem that Ed does have something of a guilty conscience, but he evades its accusations and blocks it out. (It is even censored from the movie.) Despite disingenuous attempts (he knows they won't be believed) to put himself forward as Dave's killer, Ed lets Doris take the fall for his crime because he is secretly enraged at her. When Doris hangs herself with the belt from the dress Ed brought her to wear in court, it is a sign pointing to Ed's responsibility for her death. Finally, Ed hides his sexual interest in Birdy behind a story of his pure love for her music and, when she gives him oral sex, he crashes the car rather than admit his desire for her. The car's spinning hubcap becomes a flying saucer in Ed's mind, for his own desires are 'alien' to him. He dies never knowing himself.

BRIAN DE PALMA

Femme Fatale (2002)

Directed by: Brian De Palma
Written by: Brian De Palma
Produced by: Tarak Ben Ammar and Marina Gefter
Edited by: Bill Pankow
Cinematography: Thierry Arbogast
Cast: Rebecca Romijn (*Laure/Lily*), Antonio Banderas (*Nicolas Bardo*), Peter Coyote (*Watts*), Gregg Henry (*Shiff*)

Plot

At a Cannes film premiere, model Veronica wears a diamond bra in the shape of a serpent. As part of a daring heist, con artist Laure seduces Veronica in a bathroom stall, relieving her of her jewels which are surreptitiously switched for glass replicas. Laure then makes away with the diamonds, double-crossing her accomplices, Black Tie and Racine, who are themselves untrustworthy, both being violent macho types. Afterwards, Laure is mistaken for a lookalike named Lily, who has just lost her husband and little girl in a car accident. Laure falls asleep in Lily's bathtub but is awakened when the grief-stricken other woman comes home and uses a gun to commit suicide, with Laure as a passive witness. Laure assumes the dead woman's identity, takes a plane to America and marries a man named Watts, who seven years later becomes an ambassador, bringing Laure back to France. A photographer (Nicolas) takes her picture and sells it to the tabloids. Laure meets with a mysterious brunette at an outdoor café. Just afterwards, this woman is chased and harassed by Black Tie and Racine, who throw her into the path of an oncoming truck. The two former accomplices then spot the tabloid photo of Laure. Later, when Nicolas sees Laure with a gun and fears she will try to commit suicide, he befriends her and also has sex with her. She makes it look as though Nicolas has kidnapped her and sent a ransom note to her husband. When Watts arrives with the money and Nicolas tells him the truth about his scheming wife, Laure shoots Watts and then Nicolas. But Black Tie and Racine have caught up with her: they bash her head against a bridge railing and dump her into the River Seine, where she almost drowns… except that she wakes up in the bathtub! The previous events have been a prophetic nightmare of mistakes from which she can learn to choose a better future. This time Laure saves her lookalike Lily from committing suicide, and it is Lily who boards the plane to America for a new life – but not before she leaves her deceased daughter's crystal-ball pendant with a truck driver so that he can remember his own little girl when he is on the road. It turns out that the mysterious brunette Laure meets at the outdoor café is the model Veronica, who had been Laure's secret accomplice in the robbery. The diamonds in the serpent bra were not switched; this was simply a cover for Veronica to walk away wearing them. Veronica has now fenced the jewels and gives Laure an attaché case with the money. This time around, sunlight ricochets off Laure's aluminium attaché case and onto the crystal-ball pendant hanging from the truck's rear-view mirror, which temporarily blinds the driver into swerving to hit Black Tie and Racine instead of Veronica. Both Veronica and Laure escape these deadly men, and Laure is free to start a new – and improved – relationship with Nicolas, who runs to her aid.

Comments

The brunettes Veronica and Lily can be seen as the doubles or alter egos of blonde Laure. When (or so we believe) Laure steals Veronica's jewels and Lily's identity, Laure is really stealing the possibility of a positive future from herself. In acting like a femme fatale in a film noir, Laure seals her own fate and that of her sisters/doubles: Lily commits suicide; Veronica is hit by the truck; and Laure is drowned. Indeed, as Laure watches television from a hotel-room bed before the robbery that opens the film, her naked body is reflected in the TV screen over the image of Barbara Stanwyck in *Double Indemnity*, as if Laure were assuming the identity of this femme fatale from classic film noir. But, after watching the dream-film of her desperate, criminal acts play out to its predetermined end, Laure wakes up naked in the bath, reborn as her better self. She plays 'fairy godmother' to Lily, saving her from committing suicide out of grief over her daughter's death. In so doing, Laure also mothers herself, mourning her own lost innocence so that she can move beyond committing self-destructive bad acts. And it turns out that Laure and Veronica showed sisterly solidarity during the robbery: Laure gave her back the jewels rather than stealing them from her, much as Laure gives Lily back her life rather than stealing her identity. This good deed in turn allows Lily to give the crystal-ball pendant to the truck driver, which causes a swerve in the narrative enabling Veronica to live and Laure to be freed of her dark past (the former accomplices who wanted her dead). As a TV announcer asks, 'If you could see your future in a crystal ball… or in a dream, would you change it?' 'Yep,' Laure says – and she does.

Factoid

Director Brian De Palma's own dream-work gave him the idea for Laure's revelatory dream: 'Something I discovered about my creative process is that I can be thinking about an idea and trying to figure out how to make it work and then I will fall asleep and wake up in the middle of the night with a solution. This is some kind of magical thing.'[27]

The Black Dahlia (2006)

Directed by: Brian De Palma
Written by: Josh Friedman, from the novel by James Ellroy
Produced by: Art Linson, Avi Lerner, Moshe Diamant and Rudy Cohen
Edited by: Bill Pankow
Cinematography: Vilmos Zsigmond
Cast: Josh Hartnett (*Dwight 'Bucky' Bleichert*), Scarlett Johansson (*Kay Lake*), Aaron Eckhart (*Lee Blanchard*), Hilary Swank (*Madeleine Linscott*), Mia Kershner (*Elizabeth Short*)

Plot

In 1947 Los Angeles, aspiring actress Elizabeth Short is found dead, her mouth slashed and her body cut in half. LAPD detectives Bucky and Lee are assigned to investigate the mutilation murder, which becomes known as the Black Dahlia case. Bucky is attracted to Lee's girlfriend Kay but resists for the sake of his partner – until Lee is killed, at which time Bucky and Kay's relationship begins to include lovemaking. Lee has died trying to kill Bobby DeWitt, a gangster who had once abused Kay. However, when Bucky finds out that Lee and DeWitt had been accomplices in a bank robbery and that Kay was hiding the loot, Bucky leaves Kay. Before his death, Lee had become obsessed with the Black Dahlia, and Bucky catches this obsession, even sleeping with an Elizabeth Short lookalike named Madeleine. It turns out that Lee had been blackmailing Madeleine and her family over their involvement in the Black Dahlia murder and that it was Madeleine who killed Lee. When Bucky confronts Madeleine with the truth, she claims that he will choose her over his love for Kay and his loyalty to Lee. However, Bucky shoots Madeleine dead and returns to Kay – but not before he has a horrifying hallucination of Elizabeth Short's mutilated body.

Comments

In director Brian De Palma's previous neo-noir, *Femme Fatale*, Nicolas is torn between being a voyeuristic tabloid photographer and being a good guy who really cares about Laure. In one scene, he watches her do a striptease for a lecherous bar patron. When this man attempts to assault her, Nicolas throws him off her, but then he himself has brutal sex with her (after she taunts him into doing so). In *The Black Dahlia*, Bucky is a similarly conflicted male. He wants to think of Lee and Kay as having an ideal relationship, but good girl Kay is a former mob prostitute, and Lee, rather than being purely Kay's protector, was in league with gangster DeWitt on a bank job. Lee and Kay's happy home has rotten foundations, with bank money hidden under the floor tiles. Bucky's discovery of Lee and Kay's corruption undermines his sense of self, exposing his own worst nature. When Bucky sees that Bobby DeWitt once carved his initials ('BD') into Kay's back, the good Bucky is horrified, but the bad Bucky is fascinated by this possessive branding of a woman. After all, Bucky (whose real name is Dwight Bleichert – 'DB') would like nothing more than to brand her as his own, to take Kay away from Lee. Likewise, when Bucky sees the mutilated body of Elizabeth Short or when he watches stag films of her in which she is abused from behind with a dildo, he is torn between empathising with her pain and sadistically enjoying it. (The film points to a similar ambivalence in us as viewers and in the director himself. During screen tests in which we see Elizabeth Short humiliate herself for a shot at stardom, it is De Palma's own voice as the director taunting her with such questions as 'What's a sexy girl like you so sad about?') Like Lee, Bucky always seems to be arriving too late to save women from violence, and he castigates himself for his lack of timely action. Could this be because he *can't decide* whether to help or hurt these women? In the end, Bucky does take action, shooting Madeleine to rid the world of her evil. But Madeleine is an Elizabeth Short lookalike and, when Bucky kills her, there is a sense in which he *re-enacts* the Black Dahlia murder. No wonder he is haunted by a nightmarish vision of Elizabeth Short's corpse even as he tries to return to the arms of his beloved Kay. Does he really have enough belief in her and in himself to put the past behind them and stop repeating it?

WILLIAM FRIEDKIN

The French Connection (1971)

Directed by: William Friedkin
Written by: Ernest Tidyman, from the book by Robin Moore
Produced by: Philip D'Antoni
Edited by: Jerry Greenberg
Cinematography: Owen Roizman
Cast: Gene Hackman (*Jimmy 'Popeye' Doyle*), Fernando Rey (*Alain Charnier*), Roy Scheider (*Buddy Russo*), Tony Lo Bianco (*Sal Boca*), Marcel Bozzuffi (*Pierre Nicoli*)

Plot

In Marseilles, a French detective is shot in the face by hitman Nicoli, who afterwards breaks off a piece of the man's baguette and eats it. The detective had been tailing Charnier, a shipyard owner who also regularly smuggles drugs into the United States (this is the 'French connection'). Meanwhile, in New York, narcotics cop Doyle is disguised as Santa Claus as part of an undercover surveillance operation. He and his partner Russo chase and interrogate a drug pusher, but there appears to be no heroin on the street, which means that a big shipment is probably coming soon. After tailing and wiretapping a deli owner (Boca) who somehow has big money to spend at nightclubs, Doyle and Russo suspect that Boca is actually the intermediary between a drug buyer (Weinstock) and the smuggler Charnier, who has just arrived in New York along with Nicoli. While the two Frenchmen enjoy wine and a gourmet lunch inside a warm restaurant, Doyle surveilles them from outside in the freezing cold, stuck with fast food and bad coffee. Later, the clever Charnier realises that Doyle is tailing him and slyly eludes the detective by hopping onto the subway at the very last minute and then waving from the departing train at Doyle, who is left standing on the platform. Doyle has become an annoyance, and Charnier has Nicoli attempt to kill him, firing at him with a sniper's rifle from a rooftop – but the bullets miss. When Nicoli hops aboard an elevated subway train, Doyle gives chase in a car below the tracks, swerving wildly to avoid pedestrians but colliding with some other cars during the white-knuckle pursuit. Finally catching up with him, Doyle ends up shooting the unarmed Nicoli in the back when the man attempts to flee. All the criminals meet at an abandoned factory to make the exchange of money for drugs, which have been hidden in the side panels of a car imported from France – but unbeknownst to the crooks, the cops already know the drugs are there and have followed the car to the rendezvous site. In the ensuing roundup, Doyle chases Charnier into another building. Doyle shoots at a shadowy figure and accidentally kills a fellow officer. Doyle continues his pursuit, firing another shot into the shadows. A note at the end of the film tells us that Charnier was never caught.

Comments

This film's tagline says, 'Doyle is bad news – but a good cop.' Really? Doyle's racial slurs and physical brutality may serve to intimidate suspects into snitching or confessing, just as his obsessive pursuit of his criminal quarry may lead him to break some laws in order to catch lawbreakers. As director William Friedkin notes, the 'drug racketeers' that Doyle was after 'would stop at nothing, and he discovered that he could only do his job if he didn't either'.[28] But, as Friedkin also notes, there's a 'thin line between the policeman and the criminal', a line which is 'very often crossed over'.[29] Despite the fact that his superiors and fellow cops are ready to give up on the case, Doyle's dogged pursuit of Charnier and Nicoli, which seems to become a personal grudge when the former waves goodbye to him on the subway and the latter takes a shot at him, does lead to the breakup of the drug smuggling ring. But at what cost? When Nicoli commandeers a subway train, putting the lives of its passengers at risk, Doyle commandeers a car and threatens to injure or kill pedestrians and other drivers in a high-speed chase. 'This chase embodies the character of Popeye Doyle,' Friedkin has said. 'He is totally obsessive. He will go through any obstacle to get his man and break a case. He does not care if he endangers innocent lives.'[30] Earlier, in shooting at Doyle, Nicoli has accidentally hit a woman with a baby carriage. Now Doyle in his reckless driving almost hits another woman with a baby carriage. How different are the policeman and the criminal in their reckless disregard for human life? Doyle seems to have forgotten that the point of policing is 'to protect and serve'. In the finale, while gunning for Charnier, Doyle kills one of his own men and then ends up firing into the shadows – at what could be anyone, or everyone.

Factoid

To obtain part of the footage for the chase scene, Friedkin manned the camera inside the car while a stunt man drove 80–90 miles per hour for 26 blocks, narrowly missing others in their cars who were regular city drivers with no idea of what was going on!

Cruising (1980)

Directed by: William Friedkin
Written by: William Friedkin, from the novel by Gerald Walker
Produced by: Jerry Weintraub

Edited by: Bud Smith
Cinematography: James Contner
Cast: Al Pacino (*Steve Burns*), Paul Sorvino (*Capt Edelson*), Karen Allen (*Nancy*), Richard Cox (*Stuart Richards*), Don Scardino (*Ted Bailey*)

Plot

New York City. A tugboat crewman finds a severed arm in the river. A stranger picks up a gay man in a leather bar, takes him to a hotel for sex and knifes him repeatedly in the back. Police captain Edelson assigns hetero cop Steve Burns to go undercover, posing as a gay decoy to trap the serial killer. After cruising the parks and bars, Burns returns to make love to his girlfriend Nancy, but he finds himself either overcompensating to prove his heterosexuality or growing estranged from her as he is thinking of men and leather. While prowling the night in his assumed gay identity, Burns appears to be attracted to another man (who tells him that 'that bulge in your pants ain't a knife') and he seems to lose himself by joining in the wild dancing at an S/M club. In the meantime, two additional men fall victim to the serial stabber, one in a park and another in a peep-show booth. Burns suspects a man named Skip Lee, whose job as a waiter at a steakhouse means that he has access to knives like the murder weapon. The police wire a hotel room, and Burns uses himself as bait so that they can catch Lee in the act. The wire goes dead, but when police rush in to save Burns, he does not seem to have been in any danger from Lee, who has no knife and later maintains his innocence despite a brutal interrogation. However, another clue leads Burns to surveille a suspect named Richards and then to lure him into the park. When Burns comes on to him and Richards pulls a knife, Burns stabs him first. The police have Richards' fingerprint on a coin from the peep show but, while recovering in the hospital, he denies ever killing anyone. Meanwhile, another man (Ted Bailey) is found hacked to death, and suspicion falls upon a jealous boyfriend (Gregory). However, the cop on the case (DiSimone) was earlier seen coercing oral sex from a transvestite and cruising the parks and bars, so he too may be a suspect. Finally, Burns himself, as part of his undercover identity, had rented the apartment next door to Ted and grown close to him: could Burns have been Ted's killer? In the end, once relieved of his undercover duties, Burns returns to Nancy and seems ready to resume his confident hetero identity. However, as Nancy tries on his discarded leather jacket and cap, Burns gazes intently at himself in the mirror, 'wondering who in the hell he really is'.[31]

Comments

What is most distinctive about this neo-noir is that the detective begins to question his own *sexual* identity. Some will see the film as linking homosexuality with sadomasochism and ultimately with murder, and they will see Burns as being drawn into a dark netherworld of depravity and death. When Burns is dancing orgiastically at an S/M club, another man is being sodomised with a fist while a third man, wearing the black leather mask of an executioner, looks on. By cruising the leather bars in New York City's meat-packing district (where hanging hooks and 'BEEF' signs are prominent), Burns seems to become both homosexual and homicidal, learning to treat men like meat. Does the film present homosexuality as an infectious evil? Perhaps, but what if it is homo*phobia* that is contagious? 'You know what you have to do,' Richards' father tells him, and we hear words like these – spoken by the killer but in the father's voice – right before several of the murders. Does the killer have same-sex desires but try to repress them through violence? Is he driven by his father's (or older society's) disapproval of homosexuality to kill gays? When he stabs the men from behind, he denies his own gayness but also acts out those desires in displaced form. (Note that the stabbing in the peep-show booth is interspersed with subliminal cuts of anal intercourse from a hardcore porn film.) When the killer dismembers (castrates) his victims, this could be a violently active defence against his own desire to be passively pleasured. 'I don't do anything,' Richards says; then when Burns makes a sexual advance, Richards defends against his own arousal by pulling a knife on him. It is never clear who the killer is or whether there might be more than one. (In fact, at least some of the murders do appear to be committed by different men, and the killer in the hotel murder seems to become the victim in the park murder!) This uncertainty reinforces the idea of a contagious homophobia: as long as society makes men afraid of their own gay impulses, any man might take his own fear and self-loathing out on another. Burns seems to have some inkling of this dark truth as he looks at himself in the mirror – and as his eyes, turned towards us, cause us to look at ourselves.

To Live and Die in L.A. (1985)

Directed by: William Friedkin
Written by: William Friedkin and Gerald Petievich, from the novel by Petievich
Produced by: Irving H Levin
Edited by: Scott Smith
Cinematography: Robby Muller
Cast: William L Petersen (*Richard Chance*), Willem Dafoe (*Eric 'Rick' Masters*), John Pankow (*John Vukovich*), Debra Feuer (*Bianca Torres*), John Turturro (*Carl Cody*), Darlanne Fluegel (*Ruth Lanier*), Dean Stockwell (*Bob Grimes*)

Plot

When his partner is killed, Treasury agent Richard Chance vows to stop at nothing to get the man who did it, counterfeiter Rick Masters. Chance and his new partner John Vukovich arrest Cody, Masters' mule, in possession of fake papers at the airport. During visiting hours at the prison, Cody tells Masters that Waxman, the lawyer responsible for moving his bogus bills, has been stealing from him. Masters uses his girlfriend Bianca to set a honey trap for

Waxman, then shoots the man in the groin and takes back the stolen money. Chance steals a deal book from the crime scene, allowing him and Vukovich to find out more about Masters' operation. They want to run a sting operation on Masters, but their superiors won't authorise the front money. Ruth, a woman who is Chance's informant and lover (he gets info and sex from her by threatening to revoke her parole), tips him off to an upcoming illegal diamond buy. Chance decides to 'steal real money to buy counterfeit money'. He and Vukovich kidnap the bagman and rob him, but the courier is killed in crossfire as other men shoot at Chance and Vukovich and engage them in a high-speed car chase going the wrong way on a crowded Los Angeles freeway. Later, the two partners find out that the courier they got killed was an undercover FBI agent. Posing as bankers, Chance and Vukovich pull off the sting on Masters, but due to Vukovich's momentary inattention as he reaches for handcuffs, a henchman is able to whip out a shotgun and blast Chance in the face, killing him. Vukovich pursues Masters to his downtown printing lab and finds him burning all the incriminating evidence. After a fight, Vukovich shoots Masters, causing him to drop a torch on himself and go up in flames. Vukovich then takes Chance's place with Ruth, forcing her to cooperate (in every way) with *him* now.

Comments

Chance and Masters are in some ways direct opposites. As befits his name, Masters is all about impersonal power. He tries to remain superior and invulnerable, using others to do his dirty work, including Cody, Waxman, Bianca, the henchman and a man named Rice whom Masters hires to have Cody killed. Even sex for Masters is about surveillance and control, as when he watches himself and Bianca on the videotape monitor while they are making love. In an attempt to be untouchable, Masters invests nothing of himself: it is a matter of indifference to him whether he is kissing a man or a woman (Bianca is androgynous) and he doesn't care if she sleeps with a female lover. Masters' fake money has to be perfect so that it cannot be traced back to him, and he even burns his money and his own paintings, including a self-portrait, in order to cover his trail. In the end, Masters has an ecstatic expression on his face as he burns himself up, for now, in death, he is no longer a person and is thus totally untouchable.

Chance, on the other hand, is all about personal risk. Whether it's driving the wrong way on the LA freeway or bungee-jumping off a bridge, Chance seeks out danger in order to feel the rush of having survived against the odds. With his jeans, cowboy boots and Dodge Ram, Chance is always asserting himself, even in his sexual swagger and near-rape of Ruth. Stealing in order to catch a thief, going undercover and dealing closely with crooks, Chance risks losing himself to the other side – either becoming one of the criminals himself or getting killed by them. In the end, Chance's insistence on putting his life on the line gets him shot in the face.

Despite these characters' differences, Chance's need for personal risk and Masters' desire for impersonal power are extremes that meet: they both lead to death. Note that both characters have the same first name (Richard or Rick). Writer/director William Friedkin calls Masters and Chance 'two sides of the same coin. They are both tempting death throughout the film... These are guys driving toward suicide.'[32]

Factoid

The 'wrong-way-on-the-freeway' car chase was quite innovative at the time. William Friedkin got the idea when he himself once dozed off at the wheel and woke up on the wrong side of the road with traffic headed straight for him. Many aspects of the film's car chase are deliberately disorienting. Attentive viewers will note that at one point the freeway traffic is itself reversed (for America), driving on the left side of the freeway instead of the right.

MIKE HODGES

Get Carter (1971)

Directed by: Mike Hodges
Written by: Mike Hodges, from the novel *Jack's Return Home* by Ted Lewis
Produced by: Michael Klinger
Edited by: John Trumper
Cinematography: Wolfgang Suschitzky
Cast: Michael Caine (*Jack Carter*), Ian Hendry (*Eric*), John Osborne (*Kinnear*), Britt Ekland (*Anna*)

Plot

London mob hitman Jack Carter takes the train to Newcastle to investigate the death of his brother Frank. Some say Frank was drunk and accidentally drove into the river, others that he committed suicide, but Carter believes it was murder. In a drab urban landscape of concrete slabs and rusted steel, Carter roughs up men and seduces women in order to get them to talk, all the while eluding other mobsters hired to stop him – dead, if need be. Two gangsters surprise him naked in bed with a landlady, but luckily Carter has a shotgun handy, which he holds erect and uses to walk them out the front door. Eventually, Carter learns that another gangster (Eric) had induced Frank's mistress (Margaret) to procure Frank's underage daughter (Doreen) for a pornographic film. The film was bankrolled by Eric's crime boss (Kinnear), but a rival businessman named Brumby got hold of it to use it for leverage, causing Frank to find out about his daughter's involvement. In order to stop Frank from making trouble, Eric murdered him. Once Carter has obtained this information, he turns from detection to revenge. He beats up Brumby and throws him off the top floor of a parking garage. Carter injects Margaret with an overdose of heroin and frames Kinnear for her death, while also getting the vice squad to raid his manor house for drugs and pornography. Finally, Carter forces Eric to drink a bottle of whiskey (just as Eric had done to Carter's brother Frank) before killing him and having his body dumped from a coal bucket with other waste into the sea. Carter himself is then shot dead by a sniper with a long-range rifle who has been hired by Kinnear to take him out.

Comments

It's tempting to see Carter's vengeance as righteous and to find a certain rough justice in the fact that Eric dies the same death that he imposed on Frank. But note that when Carter kills Eric, he *repeats* Eric's killing of Frank (the forced guzzling of booze, the dumping into the sea), *perpetuating* the same violence and waste of human life, which is then further continued when the sniper kills Carter. Also, we might wonder whether Carter kills others as a way of denying his own responsibility for the crimes he has committed. After all, Carter is a hitman like Eric; Carter too has killed men on the orders of his mob bosses, just as Eric killed Frank at his boss's behest. And Carter himself has done terrible wrong to Frank, having slept with his brother's wife. Indeed, Doreen could be Carter's daughter, in which case he bears some responsibility for having neglected her and allowed her to fall into nefarious hands. Moreover, Carter is a seducer and abuser of women and thus not so different from the men who lure and exploit Doreen in that pornographic film. After Carter first watches the film, he manhandles and almost drowns a naked woman in her bath. Yes, he blames her (she was in the film with Doreen) and is trying to force her to talk, but he is still committing violence against her. Similarly, when Carter later forces another guilty party (Margaret) to strip, then pins her down and uses a needle to inject her with a fatal dose of drugs, is he not a kind of rapist, worse even than the man in the film who commits statutory rape with Doreen? It's possible that Carter does realise his own culpability. In the view of writer/director

Mike Hodges, Carter 'knows he's corrupt himself, so when he kills the people who have corrupted his niece/daughter, it's to do with himself as well'. Hodges adds that 'in terms of the violence, if you look at the film carefully, it's actually on Carter's face and it reveals his own self-hatred and anger'.[33] It could be that Carter's actions are a kind of murder-suicide, that he keeps escalating the violence against others while knowing full well that it will eventually be turned back against him; that what he really wants is for all the guilty parties – himself along with them – to explode.

Croupier (1998)

Directed by: Mike Hodges
Written by: Paul Mayersberg
Produced by: Jonathan Cavendish
Edited by: Les Healey
Cinematography: Mike Garfath
Cast: Clive Owen (*Jack Manfred*), Kate Hardie (*Bella*), Alex Kingston (*Jani de Villiers*), Gina McKee (*Marion Neil*), Nicholas Ball (*Jack Manfred Sr*)

Plot

To get away from his con-man father, Jack moves from South Africa to London. Marion, Jack's live-in girlfriend, is a romantic and encourages his aspirations to be an author, but all that the publishing industry seems to want is hack work. Following up on a long-distance job tip from his father, Jack becomes a croupier at a casino, dealing blackjack and spinning the roulette wheel. Since he works nights and Marion works days, their relationship begins to deteriorate, and she doesn't like the new novel he is writing about life as a croupier, believing it to be too cynical. Ostensibly to gain material for his novel, Jack begins to take risks, breaking the casino rules. He has rough sex with a fellow employee, Bella, and he begins fraternising with Jani, one of the casino's customers. Jani is a gambler who, after a losing streak, is being threatened by gangsters to whom she owes money. Although Jack has doubts about the authenticity of her black eye and injured hand, he agrees to be the inside man on a casino robbery in order to help her pay off her debts. However, Marion intercepts a phone message from Jani to Jack, and police foil the heist. Marion tells Jack that she will turn him in to the cops unless he quits the casino, which he agrees to do, but she is then killed by a hit-and-run car. A now-cynical Jack resumes his job at the casino and takes up with the equally cynical Bella as his girlfriend. As a final turn of the screw, Jack receives a phone call from South Africa in which he learns that his father has been pulling an elaborate con trick on him all along, having known that he would take the job as croupier and then give in to Jani's temptation to 'gamble' by participating in the robbery. By the film's end, Jack has published a bestselling book called *I, Croupier*, but he does so as an anonymous author. Rather than taking any more personal risks as a gambler, Jack seems intent on remaining a detached croupier, dealing for 'the house' which always wins – the anonymous author of other people's misfortunes.

Comments

If gambling is a metaphor for life, then Jack's distant father is a kind of God (or Devil), a transcendent figure who, like 'the house' at a casino, seems to have rigged the game so that others always lose. One side of Jack wants to remain above it all like his father, to identify with that godlike position of power as 'Master of the Game'. But this cool detachment is really a defence against hot temptation and the fear of losing if he gives in to his desire to gamble. There is another side of Jack – his mirror image and fictional surrogate, Jake – who doesn't want to be a 'miserable zombie' at one remove from life. This other Jack is willing to take a risk because he has hope that he might win. Thus, although Jack suspects that Jani may be a femme fatale (and the scene where she tells him about herself is filled with distorting mirrors), he agrees to aid in the casino robbery – both to help her out and to 'gamble' against the casino. As writer Paul Mayersberg says, 'The gamblers take risks and the croupiers have no risk at all; the odds are always in favour of the casino. We have a choice in life between working in the casino or the risk-taking of being a gambler. The question arises: do you want a life of security or a life of risk? The answer is: we want both.'[34] But Jack keeps swinging between extremes. When Jani deceives him, Jack gives up all hope of romance (represented by Marion) and settles for meaningless sex (with ex-prostitute Bella). When the robbery fails and Jack loses against 'the house', he gives up any desire to win and goes back to his cold contempt for gamblers as fools. At the end, Jack believes that in his detached and superior position as a croupier he can never lose, but what he doesn't realise is that, without taking any risks, he can never really win.

I'll Sleep When I'm Dead (2003)

Directed by: Mike Hodges
Written by: Trevor Preston
Produced by: Mike Kaplan and Michael Corrente
Edited by: Paul Carlin
Cinematography: Mike Garfath
Cast: Clive Owen (*Will Graham*), Charlotte Rampling (*Helen*), Jonathan Rhys Meyers (*Davey*), Malcolm McDowell (*Boad*), Jamie Foreman (*Mickser*), Ken Stott (*Turner*), Sylvia Syms (*Mrs Bartz*)

Plot

After selling drugs at a party and then sleeping with a model, Davey is grabbed on the way home and raped in a warehouse. Back at his apartment, Davey slits his throat in the bath. Will, a former gangster who has exiled himself from his criminal past by living rough in Wales, returns to London to find out why his brother Davey killed himself. When Will learns that a rape may have caused the suicide, he works with Davey's friend Mickser to reconstruct what happened to Davey on that night. Will's former lover Helen tries to dissuade him from taking revenge and from re-entering the criminal life. Meanwhile, a crime boss named Frank Turner, who has taken over Will's old territory, fears that Will may have come to take it back. Frank's henchman Al threatens Will that he had better leave town. When Al is found in a body bag, alive but forced to wear a woman's bra and mascara, Frank assumes Will has done it. Frank hires a hitman, who holds Helen hostage and lies in wait for Will to return. Will, who has doffed his dirty clothes and gotten himself suited and booted as a gangster again, goes to confront Davey's rapist, a man named Boad. At first it seems that Will's gangster garb is only for show, a way of putting the fear of God into Boad, but just as Will is departing he turns back and shoots Boad dead. Then, though Will has earlier called Helen to say he will take her with him, he leaves town without coming to collect her. As a consequence, she is left behind with the hitman, who is unlikely to bring her to a happy end.

Comments

Boad is a wealthy man with a wife, but he is also ageing and insecure about his manhood. Davey's sexual swagger and his youthful attractiveness to women seem like a taunt to Boad, making him feel inadequate by comparison, so Boad rapes him in order to prove himself the bigger man. 'He's driven by sexual jealousy,'[35] according to director Mike Hodges, and writer Trevor Preston says that Boad has 'become obsessed with this boy he sees at parties'.[36] Boad wants to *be* Davey, but it's also possible that he wants to *have* him. Boad's description of Davey's allure – 'the women, their eyes like hands on him all the time' – suggests that Boad himself may be attracted, a desire which the rape both expresses (sexually) and denies (in its violence).

Despite his seeming self-confidence, Davey too is anxious about his masculinity, as indicated by his shadow-boxing, his womanising and his checking on his reflection in the mirror ('Devastating', he reassures himself). As the model he sleeps with tells him, 'You're not as rough as you act.' The rape undermines his manhood to the extent that he can no longer live with himself.

And what about Will, the 'hard man' gangster? When the coroner's report reveals that Davey ejaculated during the rape, Will knows that this may have been a purely physiological response, but he can't bear having others talk about whether Davey – *his* brother – was 'bent', for this becomes a negative reflection on Will's own masculinity. As Hodges says, 'The point of the film, actually, is this undermining of the machismo of all these characters.'[37] When Will uses his big gun to shoot Boad, he does it to reassert his own male dominance. The fact is that, just as Will wasn't strong enough before to stay in London and be a protective older brother to Davey, so he is weak now: he chooses to kill and go off by himself rather than face the harder challenge, which is how to make a new, non-violent life with Helen.

DAVID LYNCH

Blue Velvet (1986)

Directed by: David Lynch
Written by: David Lynch
Produced by: Fred Caruso
Edited by: Duwayne Dunham
Cinematography: Frederick Elmes
Cast: Kyle MacLachlan (*Jeffrey Beaumont*), Isabella Rossellini (*Dorothy Vallens*), Dennis Hopper (*Frank Booth*), Laura Dern (*Sandy Williams*), Dean Stockwell (*Ben*)

Plot

Small-town America. After visiting his father in the hospital, Jeffrey finds a severed ear in a field, which he takes to Detective Williams. Sandy, Williams' daughter, tells Jeffrey that she has overheard her father talking about a case involving a nightclub singer named Dorothy. Jeffrey sneaks into Dorothy's apartment and hides in her closet, where he witnesses a man (Frank) verbally humiliate and sexually violate her. Later, Jeffrey tells Sandy what he suspects: Frank has kidnapped Dorothy's husband and son and has cut off her husband's ear in order to force her to comply with Frank's sexual demands. Jeffrey returns to Dorothy's apartment. During their lovemaking, she urges him to hit her. At first he resists but then gives in to having violent sex with her. Frank arrives just as Jeffrey is leaving, and Jeffrey and Dorothy are forced to accompany Frank and his gang of thugs to a whorehouse, where Frank gets drugs from Ben, his supplier. Then, after another joy ride, Frank begins to abuse Dorothy. When Jeffrey punches him in the face to get him to stop, Frank kisses him on the mouth and then beats him within an inch of his life. After recovering, Jeffrey decides to have done with the case. He turns everything over to Detective Williams and then takes Sandy out on a date, where they share a close dance. However, upon their return, a naked and bruised Dorothy appears on the front lawn. Jeffrey tends to her, but Sandy slaps him out of jealousy – though she will forgive him. Jeffrey goes back to Dorothy's apartment, where he finds the dead body of her husband. When Frank arrives with his gun and opens the door to the closet, ready to blow Jeffrey away, Jeffrey shoots Frank first, killing him with a bullet through the forehead. Jeffrey is reunited with Sandy, and Dorothy has her son restored to her.

Comments

Jeffrey walks down a dark staircase in his own house while, in a crime film showing on the TV in the living room, one man has a gun and another man walks up a staircase. Dorothy's apartment and the field where Jeffrey finds the severed ear are both very close to Jeffrey's home. Jeffrey is Frank's 'neighbour'. The world of urban crime is right next door to small-town America, its dark other side.

When Jeffrey's father falls (from a stroke?) while watering the front lawn, the camera enters the grass to show insects in a violent turmoil underneath. Jeffrey has a nightmare in which his father's face, distorted after the stroke, dissolves into Frank's face, distorted in a violent rage. Frank *is* Jeffrey's father after the man has 'fallen' in Jeffrey's eyes, once his father's weakness, flaws and potentially violent underside have been revealed.

Sandy, the good girl in pink, emerges from darkness when Jeffrey first meets her. Jeffrey calls Sandy 'a mystery' when he is telling her about his investigation of the 'mystery' of Dorothy, the blue (abused, depressed) woman. After Jeffrey violates Dorothy's privacy by spying on her from the closet, she threatens him with a knife, and after Sandy discovers Jeffrey's dubious liaison with Dorothy (which includes hitting her during sex), Sandy slaps Jeffrey. Dorothy is Sandy's dark side, what Sandy could become if she were abused as Dorothy has been.

When Jeffrey tells her about his plan to investigate Dorothy, Sandy says to him, 'I don't know if you're a detective or a pervert.' Jeffrey watches voyeuristically from the closet as Dorothy undresses, much as Frank has her open her blue velvet robe and expose herself to his watching eyes. 'Are you a bad boy?' Dorothy asks Jeffrey, and he hits her during intercourse, much as Frank has violent sex with her. 'You're like me,' Frank tells Jeffrey. In this neo-noir, the detective is losing himself to his own dark side, turning into the pervert, the criminal. But Jeffrey also occupies the position of victim when Frank forcibly kisses him on the mouth and gives him a beating. Right after this, Jeffrey weeps as he remembers hitting Dorothy during sex, for now he knows what it feels like to be the object of such violence. It is through identification with the victim that this detective finally defeats the criminal. Earlier, a complicit Jeffrey had watched from the closet as Frank assaulted Dorothy, but in the end Jeffrey takes action, firing from the closet and killing Frank. Jeffrey's positive act enables his (good) father to recover and his (good) girl to fully forgive him.

Lost Highway (1997)

Directed by: David Lynch
Written by: David Lynch and Barry Gifford
Produced by: Deepak Nayar, Tom Sternberg and Mary Sweeney
Edited by: Mary Sweeney
Cinematography: Peter Deming
Cast: Bill Pullman (*Fred Madison*), Patricia Arquette (*Renee Madison/ Alice Wakefield*), Balthazar Getty (*Pete Dayton*), Robert Loggia (*Mr Eddy/ Dick Laurent*), Robert Blake (*Mystery Man*)

Plot

Fred suspects that his wife Renee may be cheating on him. She says she is going to stay home and read, but when Fred calls the house from the jazz club (where he plays the saxophone in a kind of jealous howl), no one answers. One night, after Fred fails to satisfy Renee in bed, he sees a Mystery Man's face superimposed over hers. On another night while Fred is out at a party, the Mystery Man walks up to him and asks him to phone home. Fred does, and the Mystery Man answers, as if he were both at the party and inside Fred's house. Fred and Renee receive a series of mysterious videotapes, which become progressively more disturbing. The first tape shows the outside of their house and approaches their front door. The second goes beyond this to show the inside of their house with Fred and Renee sleeping in their bed. The final tape reveals a bloody Fred near Renee's dismembered body. Fred is tried and sentenced to the electric chair, for it was he who actually committed Renee's murder. While on death row, Fred has a splitting headache. He has a vision of a desert cabin's *reverse* explosion, with the film running backwards so that the fiery shards come together again to form an intact structure. The next day, prison guards discover that Fred is no longer in his cell, but in his place is a younger man named Pete. Released from prison, Pete goes about his life working as a car mechanic. One day, when

Neo-Noir

a gangster named Mr Eddy drives into the garage, Pete is instantly attracted to the man's girlfriend, Alice (who looks exactly like Renee). Pete begins an affair with Alice, but the gangster grows suspicious: Pete receives a threatening phone call from Mr Eddy – and from Mr Eddy's 'friend', the Mystery Man. So that they can escape, Alice gets Pete to steal some jewels from a man (Andy), who is killed during the robbery, and Pete is disturbed when he finds out that Alice has been acting in porn films and that she seems callously indifferent to Andy's death. Alice has Pete drive out to a desert cabin to fence the jewels and, while waiting for the fence to arrive, the two begin to make love on the desert floor. However, before Pete can fully possess her, Alice abruptly leaves him and walks into the cabin, whereupon Pete turns back into Fred. When Fred enters the cabin looking for Alice, he finds the Mystery Man there, who tells him that Alice was really Renee. The Mystery Man then pursues Fred, filming him with a video camera and asking him who *he* really is. At a hotel, Fred finds Mr Eddy in bed with Alice and drags him out to the desert. The Mystery Man shows Mr Eddy videocam footage of the gangster pawing Alice, then shoots him. But in the end we see that it is Fred holding the gun; there is no Mystery Man.

Comments

Fred is sexually insecure and prone to jealous rages, but he refuses to face this fact about himself, so the truth seems to come to him from the outside in the form of the Mystery Man. When Fred sees the Mystery Man's face over Renee's and when Fred hears the Mystery Man answer the phone at home, it is because Fred fears that some unknown man is sleeping with his wife. The Mystery Man sends Fred videotapes in order to show him the truth about himself: it is Fred who threatens the marriage, Fred who dismembers his wife in a fit of jealousy. The videotapes were a warning from Fred's own unconscious about what he might do. But Fred hates video cameras because, as he explains, 'I like to remember things my own way... not necessarily the way they happened.' Thus, when Fred gets a splitting headache in prison, his head comes back together (like the reverse-exploding cabin) and reforms into that of another person: Pete. Pete is Fred's escapist fantasy, his way of denying the fact that he killed Renee and imagining that she is still alive (as Alice) and desires him. But because Fred has never dealt with his jealousy, it comes back to haunt his fantasy. Pete begins to fear that Alice is a loose woman (a porn actress), just as Fred felt that Renee was sleeping around. Alice turns from dream girl to femme fatale in Pete's mind and, when his worst fear is realised and she leaves him behind, the fantasy breaks down. In the cabin (Fred's head), the Mystery Man insists that Alice was always Renee, just as Pete was really Fred. The Mystery Man pursues Fred with a video camera and also shows Mr Eddy a video of himself being abusive towards women. As he is dying, Mr Eddy seems to recognise that he and Fred are both violently jealous men: 'You and me, mister, we can really out-ugly them sons of bitches.' But Fred still refuses to admit his own jealousy. In his mind, it is the Mystery Man who shoots Mr Eddy, whereas we see that it is really only Fred holding the gun – Fred who has killed Mr Eddy for sleeping with Alice and who will continue to act out his jealous fury until he finally acknowledges it as his own.

Mulholland Dr. (2001)

Directed by: David Lynch
Written by: David Lynch
Produced by: Mary Sweeney, Alain Sarde, Neal Edelstein, Michael Polaire and Tony Krantz
Edited by: Mary Sweeney
Cinematography: Peter Deming
Cast: Naomi Watts (*Betty Elms/Diane Selwyn*), Laura Elena Harring (*Rita/Camilla Rhodes*), Justin Theroux (*Adam Kesher*)

Plot

A black limousine winds its way up Mulholland Dr. A woman in the backseat is almost killed by a hitman but is saved when two drag-racing cars crash into the limo. The now-amnesiac woman takes refuge in a house and adopts the name 'Rita' from a movie poster of Rita Hayworth in *Gilda*. Betty, an aspiring actress, arrives at the airport, having received some words of encouragement about her Hollywood career from two grandparent types she met on the plane. When Betty finds Rita at the house, the two women form a fast friendship. Rita helps Betty rehearse her lines, which include Betty saying, 'Get out of here before I kill you.' At her studio audition, Betty gives a very convincing performance, leading a casting agent to tell her about 'a project you will kill' for. Unfortunately, Betty doesn't get the part because the director (Adam) is strong-armed by gangsters into giving the role to another woman, Camilla – 'This is the girl,' they tell him, showing him her photo. Meanwhile, Betty helps Rita with the search for her real identity. The first place they look is Rita's purse, which contains cash and a mysterious blue key. Then, spotting the nametag ('Diane') on a waitress at a diner, Rita thinks this may be her name, and she and Betty eventually find their way to an apartment where they discover a woman's corpse rotting in bed. Rita, afraid of ending up like the dead woman, is comforted by Betty, who takes her back to her place where the two women make love. However, Rita is awakened by a nightmare and takes Betty to a strange club where, after they are both moved to tears by a live singer's performance of an extraordinarily sad song, the woman is revealed to have been merely lip-syncing to a tape recording: 'It is an illusion.' Betty finds a blue box in her purse, and they return to her house where Rita opens it with her blue key. The box is empty. The fantasy of Betty and Rita has been hollowed out, proven to be an illusion, and they disappear. The real 'Betty', Diane, wakes up in bed. She remembers taking a limousine up Mulholland Dr. to meet her lover Camilla (the real 'Rita') for a party where, to Diane's horror, Camilla's engagement to Adam (the director) was announced. It turns out that Diane had earlier lost a leading role in a film to Camilla. In a fit of jealous rage, Diane meets with a hitman in the diner where she works as a waitress between acting jobs. She shows him Camilla's photo ('This is the girl') and pays him cash, and he says he'll leave a blue key as a sign when the killing is done. Later, back in her apartment, Diane stares guiltily at the blue key on her coffee table. She has a nightmarish hallucination of the grandparent types from the airport, whose words of encouragement have turned to mockery. They chase her into her bedroom where she puts a gun in her mouth and pulls the trigger – ending up as the corpse on the bed.

Comments

Is Diane's fantasy performance as sweet, helpful 'Betty' really nothing but a lie to cover up the fact that she is an evil person who had 'Rita'/Camilla killed? It would seem that 'Betty', the detective in this neo-noir, turns out to be the femme fatale! But if the point of the performance is to avoid reality, why does 'Betty' engage 'Rita' in an investigation to find out the truth? It is 'Betty' who looks up Diane's name in the phone book, who insists on going to Diane's apartment even though 'Rita' is afraid, and who climbs through a window to discover Diane's corpse. More than just an escapist fantasy, 'Betty' would also seem to be Diane's conscience driving her to face the truth about herself (that she had Camilla killed and will eventually, out of guilt, kill herself). Yet there is also a joyful, appealing aspect to 'Betty', the intrepid investigator determined to solve this puzzling case of uncertain identity. 'Betty' and 'Rita' bond like two girlhood pals in a Nancy Drew mystery. (At one point, in a classic 'friends help friends' moment, 'Rita' even links her hands to give 'Betty' a lift through the apartment window.) The 'Betty' performance isn't merely a hollow sham. It is the best of Diane – the innocent, hopeful part of her that first fell in love with 'Rita'/Camilla, before sexual jealousy and competition over movie roles led

Diane to hatred and despair. As Diane lies dying from the self-inflicted gunshot wound, she imagines 'Betty' and 'Rita' both standing together in the spotlight, both adored by applauding audiences. This is a true performance, the perfect expression of her desire for love.

INLAND EMPIRE (2006)

Directed by: David Lynch
Written by: David Lynch
Produced by: Mary Sweeney and David Lynch
Edited by: David Lynch
Cinematography: David Lynch
Cast: Laura Dern (*Nikki Grace/Susan Blue*), Jeremy Irons (*Kingsley Stewart*), Justin Theroux (*Devon Berk/Billy Side*), Peter J Lucas (*Piotrek Krol*), Julia Ormond (*Doris Side*), Grace Zabriskie (*Visitor #1*)

Plot

A Polish gypsy woman visits actress Nikki Grace to foretell that she will soon be given a role in a movie about marriage and murder. Nikki gets the part alongside actor Devon Berk, but the director (Kingsley) tells them that their movie, *On High in Blue Tomorrows*, is actually a remake of an earlier film whose German title was *Vier* (pronounced like 'fear') *Sieben* or *47*. This film, based on an old gypsy folktale, was said to have been cursed: it was never finished because its two leads were murdered. While playing the adulterous lover, Sue Blue, in the movie, Nikki begins to confuse herself with her character, falling for her co-star and saying, 'I think my husband knows about you, about us. He'll kill you and me. Damn, this sounds like dialogue from our script!' But it *is* dialogue from their script, and Nikki is in the middle of filming a scene. Later, Devon and Nikki make love – while her jealous husband (Piotrek) watches from the shadows. Nikki tells Devon about a time when she was filming another scene as Sue Blue, walked down an alley behind a marketplace and went through a door into a building, where she saw herself as Nikki reading the script of the film in which Sue is a character! Devon, who was also at the script reading, went to find out who the onlooker might be. He peered inside the window of a stage-set house, but even though she was inside looking out at him, crying out the name of Devon's character in the film ('Billy!'), Nikki could not communicate with him, for she seems trapped in the role of Sue and unable to get out. Then, looking out from the stage-set house, Nikki sees a dark street in 1930s Poland, where an earlier drama of marriage, adultery and murder is enacted, eventually ending with a woman lying on the pavement, dying from a stab wound in her side. Is this a scene from *47*, the film that Nikki is remaking – and apparently cursed to relive? In the remake, Nikki (playing Sue) tries to get Devon (playing Billy) to leave his wife for her, but the wife (Doris) slaps her. Later, a similar-looking woman (Devon's wife?) stabs Nikki in the side with a screwdriver, and she dies on Hollywood Boulevard, vomiting blood onto the golden stars in the sidewalk, her dream of achieving fame as an actress apparently over. Yet Nikki rises, and we see that she has just given a great performance in a movie death scene. After watching part of her own performance on a movie screen, Nikki goes to room 47 at the back of the theatre. When a Phantom man attacks her, she shoots him and, as he dies, she watches her own face and bleeding mouth appear over his and then dissolve. In the end, we see Nikki sitting in a blue dress with a calm smile on her face.

Comments

Actress Laura Dern, who stars in the role of Nikki, has said about her character, 'The truth is, I didn't know who I was playing – and I still don't know. I'm looking forward to seeing the film to learn more.'[38] In this neo-noir, Nikki is an investigator in search of her own identity. She seems to lose herself in her character, to re-enact the same old story, doomed to repeat the noir pattern of adultery and murder. But Nikki also *finds herself* through her performance, by projecting herself into the lives of other women and seeing the dead end to which adultery leads. As the gypsy foretold, it is 'through the alley behind' that Nikki finds 'the way to the palace' of wisdom and peace. It is by daring to look at the worst in herself that Nikki can overcome it and achieve the best. Nikki must see her alter ego Sue and *hear* what that character has to tell her about reaping what she sows. Nikki must *see herself* on screen and gain some critical distance from her own adulterous performance, recognising its ugliness and fated doom. In the end, Nikki overcomes the fear of facing herself when she goes to room 47 and shoots the Phantom, whose face and bleeding mouth are her own. When Nikki lies dying on a dark street at the end of *On High in Blue Tomorrows*, another woman comforts her by saying, 'I'll show you the light now. It burns bright forever. No more blue tomorrows. You on high now.' Nikki enacts the experience of sin and death on film so that she can be reborn as an immortal star.

Factoid

Puzzled by the 'rabbits' TV sitcom that keeps popping up during this film? Given that there are two female rabbits and one male, and given that the two females are voiced by actresses Naomi Watts and Laura Harring (who as Diane and Camilla were part of the love triangle with Adam in *Mulholland Dr.*), I would suggest that the 'secret' mentioned by the rabbits has to do with adultery.

MICHAEL MANN

Manhunter (1986)

Directed by: Michael Mann
Written by: Michael Mann, from the novel *Red Dragon* by Thomas Harris
Produced by: Richard Roth
Edited by: Dov Hoenig
Cinematography: Dante Spinotti

Cast: William Petersen (*Will Graham*), Joan Allen (*Reba McClane*), Brian Cox (*Dr Hannibal Lecktor*), Tom Noonan (*Francis Dollarhyde*)

Plot

FBI profiler Will Graham is trying to stop a serial killer, who is known as the Tooth Fairy for the bites he inflicts on his victims. To 'recover the mindset' of such a murderer, Graham consults Hannibal Lecktor, another serial killer who is now behind bars thanks to Graham's previous investigation. Before Lecktor was imprisoned, he inflicted physical and psychological damage on Graham, and a reporter named Lounds took pictures of Graham's wounds while he lay unconscious in the hospital. Now Graham has Lounds publish a slanderous story designed to bait the Tooth Fairy into attacking Graham, but the killer murders Lounds instead. Graham discovers that the Tooth Fairy and Lecktor have been corresponding and that Lecktor has given him Graham's home address, but the police put his family under protective custody. Meanwhile, it is revealed to us that the Tooth Fairy is Francis Dollarhyde, whose height, balding head and harelip have made him feel like a social outcast. Yet, suddenly, love and an end to the killing seem possible when Reba, a blind co-worker, is able to reach out to Dollarhyde. After seeing that Reba is thrilled to run her hands over the fur and teeth of a tranquillised tiger, Dollarhyde realises that she is unafraid of him, and the two make love. However, Dollarhyde's insecurities cause him to imagine that Reba is being unfaithful to him, and so he plans to kill her. Luckily, Graham has figured out who the killer is and shoots Dollarhyde, thus saving Reba and potential future victims.

Comments

When Graham goes to visit Lecktor in prison, we see matching angle/reverse-angle shots of them, each framed behind bars, as if Graham were looking into a mirror at the criminally insane killer he might become. 'You're getting deeper and deeper into this,' warns Graham's psychiatrist. The danger of Graham's job as a profiler is that, in order to get closer and closer to catching the killer, Graham must think more and more like one, staring at the dark side of himself to the point where his humanity may be lost. 'The reason you caught me,' Lecktor tells Graham, 'is that we're just alike.' Asking Graham what it felt like when he killed a man, Lecktor says, 'Didn't you really feel so bad because killing him felt so good?' When Graham finds out about the photos of his wounds that Lounds has taken, Graham slams the reporter onto the hood of a car – a revenge that feels awfully good. Later, after Lounds slights Dollarhyde's masculinity in a scurrilous news story, Dollarhyde kills the reporter in revenge, as if Dollarhyde were Graham's dark double leading him in that next step toward madness. As part of his investigation, Graham retraces the killer's steps again and again, gradually changing from 'you' to 'I' as he thinks the killer's thoughts and sees what the killer saw. (Since these are point-of-view shots, *we* too see through the eyes of the killer, and so does director Michael Mann, who served as his own camera operator and who immersed himself in investigating real-life serial killers as background research for this film.) While on a plane, Graham also looks at photos of the killer's victims, then nods off and has a dream of staring at his own wife Molly, and finally wakes up again to photos of murdered women – which scare the child in the seat next to him. At home, Graham's son is afraid to leave Graham alone with Molly: is he now seeing women through a killer's eyes? It turns out that the home movies of the victimised families that Graham has been viewing were also watched by the killer as he planned his attacks – a crucial clue to the killer's identity (he works at a film lab) that has been uncannily present within Graham all along. As this fact about the home movies is confirmed, Graham touches his own reflection in a window, growing ever closer to the killer and to his own dark side. In the end, when Graham and the killer face each other through the plate-glass window of Dollarhyde's home and

Graham smashes through the glass and shoots him, it may be that Graham is confronting and defeating his own dark side. However, it is also possible that, in killing the killer, Graham finally becomes him, taking that joyfully vengeful last step toward total identification with Dollarhyde. In the Director's Cut, Graham then pays a visit to the next family Dollarhyde has planned to kill. Ostensibly, Graham is there to tell them they are safe, but he is filmed in a way that makes him seem strange and potentially threatening, and his words – 'I just stopped by to see you' – are not necessarily reassuring because we don't know whose eyes he's looking through.

Collateral (2004)

Directed by: Michael Mann
Written by: Stuart Beattie
Produced by: Michael Mann and Julie Richardson
Edited by: Jim Miller and Paul Rubell
Cinematography: Dion Beebe and Paul Cameron
Cast: Tom Cruise (*Vincent*), Jamie Foxx (*Max*), Jada Pinkett Smith (*Annie*), Mark Ruffalo (*Fanning*), Bruce McGill (*Pedrosa*), Javier Bardem (*Felix*)

Plot

To get from the airport to her office building in downtown Los Angeles, federal prosecutor Annie is transported by cab driver Max. The two flirt, but Max is too timid to ask for her phone number (she gives it to him anyway), just as he is not confident enough to launch the limo business he has talked for years about starting. Max's next taxi passenger turns out to be a contract killer, Vincent, who takes Max hostage and forces him to drive to the location of each victim on a hit list. This list of targets is on Vincent's laptop computer, which he carries inside a briefcase. One by one, Vincent is bumping off the five witnesses scheduled to give evidence against a drug cartel. But Max gradually grows more and more assertive in his efforts to stop

Vincent, including tossing the killer's briefcase into oncoming traffic and deliberately crashing the cab. (With no more cab to drive, Max clearly won't be putting his future life on hold for another 12 years.) Vincent has taunted Max about not phoning the woman who gave him her number, but Max does finally call her – when he finds out that she is the fifth name on Vincent's hit list. (As director Michael Mann has noted, 'In the end, Vincent actually becomes an agent for the liberation of Max... to act.')[39] And when Max's cell phone dies, he takes further action, running to Annie's office building to wound Vincent just as the killer is about to shoot her. Max and Annie escape into LA's subway system with Vincent in hot pursuit, and Max is finally compelled to kill Vincent in order to save Annie's life and his own.

Comments

Vincent acts, but he takes no personal responsibility for his actions. Asked if he killed his first victim, Vincent says, 'No. I shot him. Bullets and the fall killed him.' Fatalistic and nihilistic, Vincent considers himself to be no more than an insignificant speck in an indifferent cosmos; his killings are merely part of the universal meaninglessness. What Vincent says about Los Angeles is true of his attitude towards the world: 'When I'm here, I can't wait to leave. Too sprawled out, disconnected... Nobody knows each other.' Vincent tells about a man who died on the subway and travelled round and round the city with none of the other passengers even noticing. In a telling irony, Vincent is in exactly this position at the end of the film after Max shoots him and leaves his dead body on a departing subway car. But, in showing callous indifference towards humanity, Vincent has made his lonely death into a self-fulfilling prophecy. He has pushed away – or killed – all the people who could have cared about him.

In the beginning, Max himself seems similarly isolated from the world, closed off in his perfectly clean cab and dreaming of a tropical island on a picture postcard, which he gazes at to avoid having to deal with the messy chaos of the city outside. But this chaos comes crashing in on Max in the form of a dead body that drops onto his cab, forcing Max to decide that he cares enough about the people of this city to try to save them from Vincent's violence. Max even crashes his cab, finally removing his protective shell and entering the fray to fight for Annie's life. Max's attitude towards the city is really the opposite of Vincent's. 'It's my home,' Max says, and in driving from place to place, he sees the people of this city as potentially connected, just as the aerial shots of LA's freeways show the different Latino, Anglo, black and Korean zones as all intersecting. Max feels responsible for all these people, as they are to each other, and he proves that any one of them could act to save another, as he succeeds in saving Annie. Indeed, Max's empathy is so strong that, for him, shooting Vincent feels like shooting himself. The film has Max and Vincent point guns at and shoot each other through a glass door, as if Max were shooting at his own mirror image – a fellow human being. And, when Vincent's head slumps as he dies seated on the subway, Max also bows his head in mourning as he is sitting across from Vincent. Even the death of someone like Vincent does not go unnoticed.

Factoid

80% of the film was shot on high-definition digital video, allowing great depth of field even under the low-light conditions of night shooting. Thus, both what's inside and what's outside of Max's cab are often visible and in focus, showing how he is always potentially connected with the people of this city.

Miami Vice (2006)

Directed by: Michael Mann
Written by: Michael Mann, from the TV series created by Anthony Yerkovich
Produced by: Michael Mann and Pieter Jan Brugge

Edited by: William Goldenberg and Paul Rubell
Cinematography: Dion Beebe
Cast: Colin Farrell (*Sonny Crockett*), Jamie Foxx (*Ricardo Tubbs*), Gong Li (*Isabella*), Naomie Harris (*Trudy Joplin*), Ciarán Hinds (*FBI Agent Fujima*), Justin Theroux (*Zito*), Barry Shabaka Henley (*Castillo*), Luis Tosar (*Montoya*), John Ortiz (*José Yero*)

Plot

Miami cops Crockett and Tubbs are interrupted in the middle of a sex-trafficking sting by a phone call from an old informant, Alonzo. White supremacists have taken Alonzo's wife hostage and compelled him to give up the names of undercover FBI agents, who are subsequently shot when a drug bust goes bad. When Alonzo finds out that his wife has been murdered, he kills himself by walking into oncoming traffic. Crockett and Tubbs themselves then go undercover, posing as smugglers transporting illegal product from South America to south Florida for drug kingpin Montoya. During this time, Crockett has an affair with Isabella, Montoya's mistress and business manager. But José Yero, Montoya's middleman, is jealous of the affair and suspects that Crockett cannot be trusted. Yero has white supremacists kidnap Tubbs's girlfriend Trudy and hold her hostage. Crockett and Tubbs arrive in time to shoot the Aryan Brothers and free Trudy, but Yero detonates a bomb from a remote location and Trudy is severely injured in the blast. Then, when the undercover cops meet with Yero to bust him for drugs, they discover that he is holding Isabella at gunpoint. Will she suffer the same fate as Alonzo's wife or Tubbs's girlfriend? In the ensuing gun battle, Tubbs manages to blow away Yero, and Crockett is able to save Isabella and drive her away from the scene of assault-weapon carnage. In the end, the two decide that they must separate: Isabella goes into hiding so that she will not be arrested by the police or killed by Montoya's gang, and Crockett returns to his job as a cop.

Comments

This film's first shot is underwater, a symbol for how deep undercover Crockett will go, to the point where his partner Tubbs has to warn him, 'There's undercover and then there is "Which way is up?"' Crockett gets close to Isabella as a way of infiltrating the drug cartel, but is he also falling for her and thus making himself vulnerable? *She* could be falling for *him* or merely insinuating herself to gather inside information which could be used to hurt him. Ironically, Crockett first hits on Isabella because he is feeling cocky after successfully passing as a smuggler. Conquering her would be his 'next coup', proving that he is hard, 'Teflon-coated',[40] invulnerable. Yet, precisely because Crockett is operating under the protection of a fabricated identity, he takes risks he wouldn't expose himself to in real life. Where he usually engages in only casual affairs, here Crockett allows himself to become wholly intimate with Isabella and experiences true love as a result of his false identity. When the two of them take a speedboat to Cuba where they drink mojitos, dance the salsa and make love, it is as though they briefly find a place apart – away from Miami where he is a cop and from South America where she is a criminal. They infiltrate each other to the point where their undercover romance becomes real. And yet, as director Michael Mann has said, 'It's only in their fabricated identities... that this romance can exist.'[41] Once Crockett returns to being a cop, it will be his duty to arrest Isabella. So, before this happens, Crockett commits one more crime as an undercover crook: he aids and abets Isabella's escape from the law – and from himself.

Factoid

Isabella says the same thing to Crockett that Graham's wife Molly said to him in *Manhunter*: 'Time is luck.' Mann's handheld camera with its tight shots of the characters captures the intimacy and immediacy of every passing moment.

CHRISTOPHER NOLAN

Following (1998)

Directed by: Christopher Nolan
Written by: Christopher Nolan
Produced by: Christopher Nolan, Jeremy Theobald and Emma Thomas
Edited by: Gareth Heal and Christopher Nolan
Cinematography: Christopher Nolan
Cast: Jeremy Theobald (*The Young Man*), Alex Haw (*Cobb*), Lucy Russell (*The Blonde*)

Plot

The film cuts back and forth among three different timelines, each indicated by a change in how the protagonist looks: greasy, clean-shaven or bruised. However, for the convenience of the viewer, this plot summary presents events in chronological order. In present-day London, (greasy) Bill is a would-be writer who follows people to gather material for his characters. Voyeurism turns to breaking and entering when Cobb, a burglar whom Bill has been following, has him tag along on robberies. Bill adopts Cobb's distinctive methods and even starts to look (clean-shaven) and dress like him. After one burglary in which they take some ladies' underwear, Bill starts to follow the blonde woman who occupies the apartment. Bill falls for her and agrees to steal some pornographic photos of her that her jealous ex-boyfriend, a club owner, is keeping in his office safe. An angry Cobb beats up Bill when he finds out that Bill has become personally involved with one of the robbery victims and is planning a risky job on her behalf. (Bruised) Bill steals money and photos from the safe, striking a guard with a hammer. But the pictures are not pornographic; they're mere passport photos! Bill confronts the blonde with her lie, and she admits that Cobb is her boyfriend and that the two of them have been framing Bill. The police suspect Cobb of having killed an old woman with a hammer during one of his burglaries. Cobb and the blonde have turned Bill into a burglar in order to throw suspicion off Cobb. However, after Bill leaves, the blonde is killed with a hammer by Cobb. It turns out that Cobb has in fact been framing Bill – but for the blonde's murder, which Cobb now commits as ordered by the club owner. And, indeed, since all the evidence (including the hammer and the blonde's underwear) points to Bill as the killer, the police don't believe his story that he is the victim of a set-up.

Comments

Bill wants to be more than just an anonymous face in the crowd, a follower who shadows other people's lives. The Batman sign on Bill's door shows that he wants to be the hero of this story, a fearless man of action who saves the blonde damsel in distress. Bill is so ready to believe Cobb because he wants to *become* him and, soon enough, the freshly shaved and nattily dressed Bill has 'taken on some of the attributes of Cobb', the 'confidence' and 'aggressiveness'[42] that enable Bill to chat up the blonde in a bar. And Bill is so willing to believe *her* because he wants to be her saviour, to prove that he can rob the safe on his own and retrieve those dirty photos to restore his lady's honour. It is because Bill has so little sense of self that he makes the perfect patsy. Rather than being a leader among men or a stealer of women's hearts, Bill merely *follows* Cobb and *is seduced by* the blonde. They take Bill's desire to 'be somebody' and use it against him, turning him into a nobody – just another victim with a battered face. And Bill may be at least partly deserving of punishment for having deluded himself into thinking he's a hero rather than a voyeur, robber and near-murderer (he took a hammer to that guard). There is a certain poetic justice in the fact that Bill is accused of having committed murder with a hammer (the killing of the blonde), just as there is in the fact that the blonde ends up hammered to death like the old lady for whose murder she had been trying to frame Bill. And if we as viewers delude ourselves about our own knowledge and power – if 'we start… thinking we know a lot more about what's going on than [Bill] does'[43] when we see Cobb and the blonde conspiring against him – then *we* are punished for *our* presumption when we find out that Cobb has been plotting against her as well.

Memento (2000)

Directed by: Christopher Nolan
Written by: Christopher Nolan, from the short story 'Memento Mori' by Jonathan Nolan
Produced by: Jennifer and Suzanne Todd
Edited by: Dody Dorn
Cinematography: Wally Pfister
Cast: Guy Pearce (*Leonard*), Carrie-Anne Moss (*Natalie*), Joe Pantoliano (*Teddy Gammell*)

Plot

Memento is told in black-and-white segments moving forward in time, intercut with colour segments moving backward in time. In terms of the overall timeline, the black-and-white segments end where the colour ones begin. For this plot summary, I have reorganised the film's events into chronological order.

Since the rape and murder of his wife, Leonard has suffered from short-term memory loss. After talks with Teddy, who claims to be an undercover cop, Leonard is convinced that his wife's killer was a drug dealer named Jimmy Grantz. Leonard meets Jimmy at an abandoned house and kills him. Teddy arrives and tells Leonard that his wife actually survived the rape and that it was Leonard who killed her by accidentally giving her too much insulin. Ever since then, Teddy has been finding men with the initials 'JG' for Leonard to kill. But Leonard refuses to believe Teddy. Instead, he has Teddy's licence-plate number tattooed on his leg, thus deliberately setting him up to be the next 'JG' to be killed. (Teddy's real name is John Gammell.) Though Leonard has now forgotten why, he finds himself driving Jimmy's car and wearing the dead man's clothes, and a beer coaster in one of the pockets leads him to a bar where he meets Natalie, who was Jimmy's girlfriend. After testing Leonard's claims about his memory loss by spitting in his beer and then seeing him forget and happily drink it a few minutes later, Natalie seems to befriend him. But then she manipulates Leonard by provoking him to hit her and, as soon as he has forgotten, telling him she was beaten up by a man named Dodd, whom she wants Leonard to get rid of for her. (Dodd, who was Jimmy's partner, has been hassling Natalie for Jimmy's money and drugs.) Natalie also 'helps' Leonard match the licence-plate number on his leg to Teddy. (She is using Leonard to take revenge on Teddy, whom she blames for Jimmy's death.) Leonard and Teddy drive out to the same abandoned house where Leonard killed Jimmy, and despite Teddy's protestations ('You don't know me. You don't even know who you are.'), Leonard kills him.

Comments

Is Natalie a friend and lover or a femme fatale? Is Teddy a helpful sidekick or a deceptive villain? These ambiguities are typical of film noir, but *Memento* goes one better: is Leonard the victim, the detective, or the killer? It could be argued that Leonard plays the cool detective in order not to be a disoriented victim. By methodically following the clues in order to catch the killer, Leonard tries to master the trauma of his wife's murder, to regain power and control over a situation in which he had earlier been helpless. But if Leonard just keeps on killing an endless series of men with the initials 'JG', then he is not a master detective but the victim of an obsessive and futile search for revenge. (He is also the victim of Teddy's and Natalie's manipulations.) And we must not forget(!) that Leonard himself could be the killer he seeks. As writer/director Christopher Nolan has said,

'What I like about the film noir genre is that it really lends itself to a more extreme storytelling approach. Flashbacks, subjective truth.'[44] Whenever this reverse-chronology film takes a step backwards in time, another assumption that Leonard has made about the truth of events is challenged as possibly false, for his memory is shown to be potentially unreliable. He remembers a man named Sammy Jankis who, due to short-term memory loss, gave his diabetic wife too many insulin injections, but is Sammy a 'screen memory', allowing Leonard to hide the truth about what he himself did? Does Leonard's leg tattoo of Teddy's licence-plate number tell part of the truth (an injection with a needle) while denying Leonard's own guilt and falsely pointing to Teddy as the killer? Perhaps Leonard's real tragedy is not that he has lost his memory, but that he is afraid to find it.

The Dark Knight (2008)

Directed by: Christopher Nolan
Written by: Jonathan and Christopher Nolan, based on characters created by Bob Kane
Produced by: Charles Roven, Emma Thomas and Christopher Nolan
Edited by: Lee Smith
Cinematography: Wally Pfister
Cast: Christian Bale (*Bruce Wayne/Batman*), Heath Ledger (*The Joker*), Aaron Eckhart (*Harvey Dent/Two-Face*), Michael Caine (*Alfred*), Maggie Gyllenhaal (*Rachel Dawes*), Gary Oldman (*Gordon*)

Plot

The Joker robs mob money from a bank with the help of a gang of men, whom the Joker gets to kill each other off so that only he is left with the loot. This theft, along with his own kill-crazy fearlessness, allows the Joker to take control of the crime syndicate. When Batman kidnaps corrupt businessman Lau from Hong Kong and takes him back to Gotham City to testify against the mob, the Joker threatens to kill Gotham's citizens unless Batman unmasks himself. However, it is district attorney Harvey Dent who claims to be Batman and turns himself in as a vigilante. This is revealed to be part of a plot to use Dent as bait for the Joker so that Batman can catch the fiend, which he does. But getting himself arrested was part of the Joker's counterplot so that he is able to get into jail to kill Lau and prevent him from testifying. In addition, during interrogation the Joker informs Batman that he must choose whether to save the woman he loves (Rachel) or the man who symbolises justice for Gotham City (Dent): the Joker has wired both of them to detonators in separate locations and Batman only has time to rescue one of them before the bombs go off. Batman goes to rescue Rachel, but the Joker has given him the wrong address, so Dent is saved (though one half of his face is horribly burned), while Rachel is blown up. Next, the Joker wires two ferries with explosives and tells the passengers on each ferry that they must use the detonators he has given them to blow up the people on the other boat or he will kill everyone on both boats. But the people do not turn on each other out of fear; they resist killing others to save themselves. And Batman captures the Joker – without killing him.

Comments

In *Batman Begins* (2005), the boy Bruce feels responsible for the death of his parents because it was his fear of bats that prompted them to leave the theatre and enter an alley where they were shot by a mugger. When Bruce turns himself into Batman, he becomes what he fears so that he can frighten and fight back against all criminals like the mugger. But Bruce as Batman may still be *driven by* fear, lashing out at others to deny his own sense of guilt, taking revenge for his own personal reasons and satisfaction. As Alfred the butler warns him, 'You're getting lost inside this monster of yours... It can't be personal or you're just a vigilante.' Bruce comes to realise that, if he had actually gunned down the mugger outside a courtroom, he would have been essentially no different from the mugger himself who shot his parents. 'I was a coward with a gun,' Bruce says, admitting that he would have been acting out of fear. 'Justice is about more than revenge.' By becoming Batman, Bruce must *conquer* his fear so that his actions are no longer motivated by personal vendetta but by higher justice. When criminals release an airborne hallucinogen that makes citizens lash out in terror at each other, Bruce must remember that 'there's nothing to fear but fear itself'. The criminals must fear Batman, but Bruce has to make the public believe that, if they trust each other, they will bring out each other's goodness.

In *The Dark Knight*, Batman is again sorely tempted to substitute his own vengeance for any higher law. During the interrogation scene, the Joker makes taunting remarks about Batman's personal feelings for Rachel, the girlfriend of his best friend Harvey Dent. In this way, the Joker lures Batman into torturing and almost killing him, in an attempt to get Batman to break his own moral code and commit murder. As writer/director Christopher Nolan explains, 'We show Batman going too far. We show him effectively torturing someone for information because it's become personal' – a 'moment where his rage might spill over and he would break his rules'.[45] But Batman retains his faith in justice and does not murder the Joker. Instead, it is ironically Harvey Dent, once the symbol of justice as Gotham City's district attorney, who loses faith in the law. Unable to save his beloved Rachel from the Joker's deadly explosion, Dent can no longer believe in the law's ability to bring criminals to justice. Instead, he pursues his own personal vendetta and begins to kill almost indiscriminately, flipping a coin to decide who lives or dies. Dent thus becomes just like the Joker, the haphazard killer he hates. However, after Dent falls to his death, Batman lets himself be blamed for Dent's crimes so that the public will still believe in their former district attorney as a symbol of justice. The tragedy here is not just the terrible burden that must be carried by Batman, but also the fact that people still need a hero at all because they are not strong enough to be heroes themselves.

STEVEN SODERBERGH

The Underneath (1995)

Directed by: Steven Soderbergh
Written by: Sam Lowry (Steven Soderbergh) and Daniel Fuchs, from the novel *Criss Cross* by Don Tracy
Produced by: John Hardy
Edited by: Stan Salfas
Cinematography: Elliot Davis
Cast: Peter Gallagher (*Michael Chambers*), Alison Elliott (*Rachel*), William Fichtner (*Tommy Dundee*)

Plot

The film cross-cuts among events in three different time periods in the life of Michael Chambers. To aid the viewer, these events are here presented in chronological order. 1. Some years ago (when he has a beard), Michael's compulsive gambling leads him to neglect his mother, his brother David and his girlfriend Rachel. When a losing streak burdens him with debts he cannot pay, Michael skips town. 2. Michael (now clean-shaven) returns to town. Rachel has started seeing a small-time gangster named Tommy, but Michael convinces her to run away with him, arguing that *she* is what matters to him now. However, she is a no-show at their rendezvous. Later, Michael learns that David threatened Rachel to get her to stay away from him and that Rachel subsequently married Tommy. Nevertheless, Michael continues to pursue Rachel and, when the violently jealous Tommy discovers them talking together, Michael invents a cover story, explaining that he had approached Rachel only as a way of getting Tommy's help with a bank robbery. 3. In the present, Michael is a security guard driving an armoured car to the bank, followed (in accordance with his plan) by a white van full of robbers. Unexpectedly, though, two people Michael cares about – his father-in-law (Ed) and a bank teller (Susan) – are endangered by the robbery, and Michael is shot trying to save them. Michael is then abducted from the hospital and brought to Tommy and Rachel, who prepare to kill him. However, Rachel slips the gun to Michael and, when Tommy comes at him, Michael shoots the man. But Rachel, instead of running away with Michael, abandons him, skipping town with the money – though we see that she is being followed by the robbers in the white van, so she is unlikely to get away with it.

Comments

Although director Steven Soderbergh has expressed some disappointment over this film, it remains an ambitious attempt to complicate the genre (Soderbergh has called it 'a revisionist nonlinear noir movie') and to add European complexities of character and motivation to an American action picture: 'to splice an armoured-car-heist movie together with Antonioni's *Red Desert*.'[46] Michael has neglected his girlfriend in the past, as when he watches sports on TV (he has bet money on the game) while ignoring Rachel's practice for an audition. (She acts the part of a TV lotto announcer, as if she were desperately trying to enter his world of televised gambling.) Michael was already absent from Rachel's life – 'I feel like you're somewhere else. You're not very present tense' – even before he abandons her. When Michael returns, it might seem as though he has learned his lesson, wanting nothing else now but to be with Rachel. But is it Rachel he sees or some idealised version of her; the Rachel he could have had if he hadn't ruined their previous relationship? As Soderbergh says, 'I don't think Michael is able to delineate between the idea of putting the relationship with Rachel back together – and whether he's just enamoured of that idea – and the reality of it. And I think she exploits that confusion.'[47] While Michael is dreaming of a romantic reunion with his ideal Rachel, the real Rachel has been forever changed by his gambler's neglect and abandonment of her –

to the point where she, now devoid of trust or hope, greedily takes all the money and abandons *him*.

The way the film keeps flashing back to earlier periods in Michael's life may create the impression that he cannot escape his past, that he is predestined to lose. Even as Michael drives the armoured car in the present towards what he hopes will be a successful robbery, the flashbacks to past failures – along with the images of him 'framed' in the car window and the colour filter making his face a sickly green – give a sense that he is doomed to disaster. Michael could almost say what the protagonist of *Criss Cross*, the classic 1949 noir on which this film is based, says: 'From the start, it all went one way. It was in the cards, or it was fate or a jinx, or whatever you want to call it.' But, in blaming fate, Michael would be once again evading responsibility for his own choices. As Soderbergh explains, 'I made a gambler out of the character, so his life is dependent on luck, but at the same time I show that he has the choice to be a gambler or not. And that he ends up a prisoner of his choice.'[48] How curious that the story Michael makes up to avoid Tommy's jealous wrath is a plan to rob a bank! Didn't anything less risky occur to him? No, because even though he won't admit it to himself, Michael has once again put himself in a situation where he has to take a big gamble. Michael claims that his sole interest this time around is Rachel, but he is still as obsessed with risk and cash as he was when he had Rachel excite him by using her foot to take gambling winnings out of his lap. 'Feels almost as good as you,' she said, but Michael wasn't thinking so much about her: 'God, I love betting!' And risk remains his first love – right up until the end.

Out of Sight (1998)

Directed by: Steven Soderbergh
Written by: Scott Frank, from the novel by Elmore Leonard
Produced by: Danny DeVito, Michael Shamberg and Stacey Sher
Edited by: Anne V Coates

Cinematography: Elliot Davis
Cast: George Clooney (*Jack Foley*), Jennifer Lopez (*Karen Sisco*), Ving Rhames (*Buddy Bragg*), Don Cheadle (*Maurice Miller*), Dennis Farina (*Marshall Sisco*), Albert Brooks (*Richard Ripley*)

Plot

Coincidentally, federal marshal Karen Sisco is present just as bank robber Jack Foley and his partner Buddy are breaking out of prison. She tries to intercept them, but they overpower her, and Jack and Karen spend some time squeezed together in the trunk of a getaway car. Later, Karen joins the task force assigned to recapture the prison escapees. Seated in the lobby of a Miami hotel, she sees Jack wave to her from an elevator, but she doesn't call the cops on him. After tracking him to Detroit, Karen converses with Jack in a cocktail lounge and the two make love in her hotel room. Jack and Buddy are planning to rob the mansion of financier Richard Ripley, whom they know from prison. But some other former prison inmates, led by the vicious Maurice, insist on taking part in the home invasion, and Karen is also tipped off about the heist. Jack and Buddy locate the uncut diamonds hidden in the house and are making their escape when Jack decides to turn back in order to save Midge, Ripley's girlfriend, from being raped and killed by Maurice's gang. Maurice and Jack fight, and Karen arrives just in time to shoot Maurice dead. Jack would rather Karen shoot him than be taken back to prison, and she does – but only in the leg. Jack is recaptured and on the way to being incarcerated again when he discovers that Karen has arranged for his fellow passenger to be a convict who explains how he has successfully escaped from prison nine times...

Comments

In director Steven Soderbergh's previous neo-noir, *The Underneath*, Michael and Rachel suffered from a tragic case of bad timing: he was a reckless gambler while she wanted to settle down, and when he finally matured enough to seek a steady romance, she had turned wild and untrustworthy. By contrast, in *Out of Sight*, Jack and Karen eventually get their timing right. At first it seems as though the two are incompatible. After all, he is an outlaw and she represents the law. A career criminal, he seems destined to die in a shootout or to wind up in prison again, and her job is to ensure one of these fates for him. 'This is not going to end well,' Karen tells him; 'these things never do.' Jack too fears that their romance will end before it has even begun: 'It's like seeing someone for the first time… You look at each other and for a few seconds there's this kind of recognition… The next moment the person's gone, and it's too late to do anything about it.' But the force of their desire for each other enables Jack and Karen to take a 'time-out', to lift themselves out of the fatalistic noir plot and make time for a happily-ever-after romance. They do this by departing from their set roles. Jack kidnaps Karen but only so that he can spend some time close to her in the car's trunk. Karen pursues Jack because she is interested in capturing him *for herself*. Jack and Karen extend their cat-and-mouse game for as long as possible so that they can continue their interaction and not bring it to a predetermined bad end. As Karen chases Jack from Miami to Detroit, the hues darken from coral-coloured pastels to gun-metal blues as the plot seems to take an inevitable turn for the worse, but even in snowy-cold Detroit the couple find the time to communicate verbally (in the cocktail lounge) and sexually (in the hotel bed). As the two make love, a freeze-frame lifts them out of time, preserving their intimacy forever. And at the end, by orchestrating Jack's future escape from prison, Karen ensures that there will be no end to their romance since she will be 'required' to pursue him again once he gets out. Despite their roles as cop and criminal, Karen and Jack are ultimately compatible. As a risk taker herself, she is attracted to bad boys, and he, though an outlaw, is a non-violent one: he's never forced himself on a woman or used a gun when robbing a bank.

After taking Karen's gun from her during the kidnapping, Jack later leaves it on a pillow once they have made love, returning her power to her. And Karen, after shooting Jack in the leg, ensures that he can escape and gives him back his Zippo lighter, restoring his manhood and their romantic spark.

The Limey (1999)

Directed by: Steven Soderbergh
Written by: Lem Dobbs
Produced by: John Hardy and Scott Kramer
Edited by: Sarah Flack
Cinematography: Ed Lachman
Cast: Terence Stamp (*Wilson*), Lesley Ann Warren (*Elaine*), Luis Guzman (*Eduardo Roel*), Barry Newman (*Jim Avery*), Peter Fonda (*Terry Valentine*)

Plot

Cockney ex-con Wilson flies to California to take revenge on the man responsible for the death of his daughter Jenny. Wilson crashes a party at the luxury house of rock promoter Terry Valentine, and Wilson almost shoots Valentine but instead throws one of the man's bodyguards over the railing of a raised swimming pool to his death. Valentine and his entourage retreat to a Big Sur hideaway, but Wilson pursues them and makes a stealth attack on the house. In the ensuing confusion, Valentine's security chief Avery accidentally shoots Stacy, the thug he had hired to take out Wilson, and then Avery himself is shot as Avery's and Stacy's men kill each other off. Wilson holds Valentine at gunpoint and gets him to confess that he killed Jenny when she found out that he was laundering money from drug deals and threatened to turn him in to the police if he didn't stop. But, rather than shooting Valentine, Wilson just walks away and then takes a plane back to his home country.

Comments

In the party-crashing scene, Wilson imagines pointing his gun at Valentine and shooting to kill, then Wilson imagines shooting to wound, and finally he doesn't shoot at all. It is as though his mind has sifted through various possibilities in order to settle on the right course of action. The entire movie could be said to work this way. After all, it begins and ends with Wilson on a plane, remembering scenes from the past and projecting possible futures, pondering the subject of revenge. What Wilson says about deciding not to take revenge against a prison guard is also true about his decision to let Valentine go in the end: 'What I thought I wanted wasn't what I wanted... This bloke... wasn't worth my time. 'Cause you've got to make a choice: when to do something and when to let it go. ...Bide your time and everything becomes clear. And you can act accordingly.' With its flashbacks and flashforwards, its remembered and projected scenes, this film bides its time as Wilson waits to take action until after he is sure that revenge is what he really wants. Wisely, he waits long enough to decide that it is not. Now, some might say that Wilson has ample reason for revenge. The ageing and narcissistic Valentine seems to have preyed on Jenny's youthful body and spirit, much as he capitalised on the '60s youth movement and sold its soul. When Wilson sees Jenny's photo in Valentine's house, a collection of sexual figurines, and Valentine's latest girlfriend naked in the bath, Wilson is enraged at the exploitation of his daughter. But when Valentine finally confesses his guilt, Wilson realises that he himself is equally culpable in his own way. A career criminal, he has spent half his life behind bars, fatally neglecting his daughter who sought companionship in the arms of Valentine, another bad man. Moreover, Jenny loved Valentine as she had Wilson, for at various times she had threatened to turn each of them in if they didn't reform. So, rather than shoot Valentine, Wilson is forced to examine his own soul and acknowledge his shared responsibility for Jenny's death. As director Steven Soderbergh puts it, 'The result is not explosion but implosion.'[49] And yet the film ends with Wilson remembering a time when, as a younger man, he played the guitar and sang a song that won the approval of a woman. If, as screenwriter Lem Dobbs says, 'memory is the path not taken' and a way of imagining 'how could things have been different?'[50] then perhaps Wilson finds his future in his past. Having admitted his own guilt, he may now be able to turn from revenge to forgiveness and renew his life.

QUENTIN TARANTINO

Reservoir Dogs (1992)

Directed by: Quentin Tarantino
Written by: Quentin Tarantino
Produced by: Lawrence Bender
Edited by: Sally Menke
Cinematography: Andrzej Sekula
Cast: Harvey Keitel (*Mr White/Larry*), Tim Roth (*Mr Orange/Freddy*), Michael Madsen (*Mr Blonde/Vic*), Chris Penn (*Nice Guy Eddie*), Steve Buscemi (*Mr Pink*), Lawrence Tierney (*Joe Cabot*)

Plot

A heist movie in which you never see the heist, *Reservoir Dogs* focuses on the disintegration of a gang of jewel thieves after a job goes bad. But first we see the men bonding over breakfast at a diner, then walking (in slow motion) as a unit towards the robbery, with all of them wearing black suits and thin black ties. Suddenly, though, this iconic image of masculine cool gives way to a shot of one man (Mr Orange) moaning and bleeding in the backseat of a getaway car, while another man (Mr White) desperately tries to reassure him that he is not going to die. Eventually, all the members of the gang rendezvous at a claustrophobic warehouse where, in sweaty real time, they try to figure out who ratted them out to the cops (who were lying in wait for them at the diamond store). Mr White and Mr Pink beat up a captured cop to try to get him to talk and, after they leave for a time, Mr Blonde tortures the cop by cutting his ear off with a razor (while dancing to the tune of 'Stuck in the Middle with You'). Then, just as he is about to set the cop on fire, Mr Blonde is shot dead by Mr Orange. A flashback reveals that Mr Orange is an undercover agent, but when the other members of the gang arrive, he tries to convince them that Mr Blonde was the double-crosser. Eddie shoots the captured cop, and Joe (the gang boss) points a gun at Mr Orange, disbelieving his story. Mr White points *his* gun at Joe in defence of Mr Orange, and Eddie aims at Mr White. This Mexican stand-off ends in a hail of gunfire, with Joe and Eddie dead and Mr Orange and Mr White wounded. Mr Pink makes off with the diamonds, but we hear sirens and gunfire as he is shot by police outside. Mr White cradles the bleeding Mr Orange, telling him that they'll be doing time together in prison. But, when Mr Orange confesses ('I'm a cop. Larry, I'm sorry.'), Mr White gives a sobbing moan and, though told by the police to drop his gun, shoots Mr Orange in the head, whereupon the police shoot Mr White.

Comments

Reservoir Dogs is a character study of loyalty and betrayal among gangsters. To begin with, given that their 'profession' is robbery, the gang are disloyal to society, to their fellow citizens whom they rip off. According to writer/director Quentin Tarantino, the gang's 'professionalism' is really just 'a way to bullshit themselves into thinking it's a regular job, like a carpenter or a craftsperson. But being a crook is not a regular job. You are going against society... Putting guns into people's hands and having them achieve things with the threat of murder? At some point that stops being a profession' and becomes 'hooliganism.'[51] So, when the undercover agent Mr Orange lies to the gang about who he really is and betrays them to the cops, it's worth remembering that Mr Orange *is* being loyal *to society*, remaining true to his profession as a policeman. Nevertheless, Mr Orange is conscience-stricken over his personal disloyalty to Mr White, who has comforted him during his bloody suffering and who trusted him enough to take a bullet for him. Mr Orange cannot live with the sin of his personal betrayal of Mr White without confessing the truth to him, which he does even at the cost of his own life. For his part, Mr White has treated Mr Orange like a surrogate son, instructing him in how to steal, adopting him into the crime family. Mr White is thus personally invested in Mr Orange, feels his suffering when he is shot and defends him against what he believes is the gang's false accusation of betrayal. But then Mr Orange confesses. Does Mr White kill Mr Orange out of revenge for his treachery, or because he cannot bear to hear the other speak his disloyalty and would rather the other – and himself – be dead? It could be that Mr Orange and Mr White are not loyal to society or the gang in the end; instead, they form a suicide pact in order to stay loyal to each other.

Factoid

Many viewers wonder, who shot Eddie? A mistimed special effect makes Eddie seem to get hit and fall before anyone could have shot him, but slowing down the DVD reveals that Mr White, after first shooting Joe and while falling from Joe's bullet, turns and takes Eddie out with a second shot.

Pulp Fiction (1994)

Directed by: Quentin Tarantino
Written by: Quentin Tarantino
Produced by: Lawrence Bender
Edited by: Sally Menke
Cinematography: Andrzej Sekula

Get Carter (1971) directed by Mike Hodges. Metro-Goldwyn-Mayer.

Chinatown (1974) directed by Roman Polanski. Paramount.

Taxi Driver (1976) directed by Martin Scorsese. Columbia.

Blade Runner (1982) directed by Ridley Scott. Warner Bros.

Blade Runner (1982) directed by Ridley Scott. Warner Bros.

Manhunter (1986) directed by Michael Mann.
De Laurentiis Entertainment Group.

The Crying Game (1992) directed by Neil Jordan. Miramax.

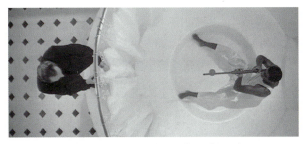

Suture (1993) directed by Scott McGehee and David Siegel.
Samuel Goldwyn Company.

Pulp Fiction (1994) directed by Quentin Tarantino. Miramax.

Fargo (1996) directed by Joel Coen. Polygram.

Lost Highway (1997) directed by David Lynch. October Films.

The Talented Mr. Ripley (1999) directed by Anthony Minghella. Paramount/Miramax.

Memento (2000) directed by Christopher Nolan. Newmarket.

Ichi the Killer (2001) directed by Takashi Miike.
Omega Project/Micott & Basara.

Mulholland Dr. (2001) directed by David Lynch. Universal.

Femme Fatale (2002) directed by Brian De Palma. Quinta Communications.

Oldboy (2003) directed by Chan-wook Park. Tartan Films.

Sin City (2005) directed by Frank Miller and Robert Rodriguez. Dimension Films.

The Dark Knight (2008) directed by Christopher Nolan. Warner Bros.

Watchmen (2009) directed by Zack Snyder. Warner Bros/Paramount.

Cast: John Travolta (*Vincent Vega*), Samuel L Jackson (*Jules*), Bruce Willis (*Butch*), Uma Thurman (*Mia*), Harvey Keitel (*The Wolf*), Tim Roth (*Pumpkin*), Amanda Plummer (*Honey Bunny*), Ving Rhames (*Marsellus Wallace*)

Plot

What would *Pulp Fiction* look like as a straightforward narrative? Here are the film's events reorganised in chronological order. Gangsters Jules and Vincent are sent by their crime boss, Marsellus, to kill some college kids who failed to return a briefcase filled with valuables (the jewels from the *Reservoir Dogs* heist?). One of the kids bursts from the bathroom and fires multiple times at the two gangsters, but all the bullets miss. After completing the hit, Jules and Vincent drive off with another one of the college boys in the backseat, and Vincent's gun accidentally goes off, splattering the boy's brains. Stopping off at a friend's house, the gangsters get advice from a fixer, Mr Wolf, on how to clean everything up before the friend's wife can come home and discover the bloody mess. Changing out of their natty suits and into shlubby shorts and T-shirts, the gangsters go to a diner for breakfast. Jules declares his belief that the bullets' missing them was a miracle and a sign that he should leave the life of crime. As his first good act, Jules refrains from killing an outlaw couple (Pumpkin and Honey Bunny) who rob the diner. Jules and Vincent return the briefcase to Marsellus at his club. Here Vincent briefly crosses paths with a boxer named Butch, who is pressured to throw his next fight so that Marsellus can win big on it. Later that night, Vincent, following Marsellus's orders, takes his boss's wife Mia out to dinner at a '50s-themed restaurant, where the two pair up on the dance floor. Afterwards, Mia overdoses on heroin (which she snorts, mistaking it for cocaine), and Vincent has to revive her with a needle of adrenaline to the heart. At the fight, Butch KOs (and actually kills) his opponent rather than taking a dive, but before he can leave town with his winnings and his girlfriend, he must return to his apartment to get his father's watch, which he does the next morning. Vincent is lying in wait for him there, but Butch catches Vincent with his pants down in the bathroom and kills him first. Driving away, Butch has a run-in with the vengeful Marsellus, who chases him to a white-supremacist pawn shop. Butch manages to escape his bonds while Marsellus is being raped by a redneck in the next room, but Butch does the honourable thing and goes to rescue Marsellus. In exchange for saving him, Marsellus forswears revenge and lets Butch get away with his winnings and his life.

Comments

These chronologically ordered events seem entertaining enough, so why does the actual film mix them up, constantly departing from a straightforward crime story? It could be that *Pulp Fiction* wants to interrupt pulp fiction, to deviate from the 'kill and be killed' plot of most noir narratives in order to avoid a dead end. Butch is a washed-up boxer about to take a dive, but his story is interrupted by a dream in which he remembers a man giving him his father's watch, symbol of his father's courage and loyalty to his comrades during the war. After waking up, Butch is inspired to stand up to his opponent in the boxing ring and then to stand by Marsellus during the redneck attack. As a result of Butch's breaking out of the cycle of violence, Marsellus spares his life and allows him to go free. (Unfortunately, Marsellus himself is still acting out the same old story, planning to 'get medieval' on the 'ass' of the redneck who raped him.)

The gangster Jules thinks it sounds cool to spout Bible verse right before he kills, but then his hit on the college boys is interrupted by a miracle (of bullets that miss him and Vincent). Jules eventually changes course and departs from this crime story, deciding to spare lives (as his was spared) and to become a true preacher.

Vincent, however, will not be detoured from the dead-end gangster plot. The bullets missed him too, but Vincent believes they 'accidentally' misfired, and as he is arguing with Jules about it, Vincent's own gun 'accidentally' goes off, killing the boy in the backseat. But if Vincent bears some responsibility for the latter (he *was* pointing a loaded gun at the boy), isn't it possible that a higher power is responsible for the former (a miracle)? Vincent almost seems to realise this when, after Mia overdoses on his drugs, he is able to revive her with an injection. Vincent takes responsibility for her, and she is saved by his potential love for her (his needle to her heart) and by some kind of miracle. But the next day finds Vincent still playing the hitman in a crime drama, still reading pulp fiction in the bathroom as he waits for his next target (Butch) to arrive. Only now, Vincent is at the end of the story. When Butch fires, the bullets don't spare Vincent this time.

NEO-NOIR DISCOVERIES

Seconds (1966)

Directed by: John Frankenheimer
Written by: Lewis John Carlino, from the novel by David Ely
Produced by: John Frankenheimer and Edward Lewis
Edited by: David Newhouse and Ferris Webster
Cinematography: James Wong Howe
Cast: Rock Hudson (*Antiochus 'Tony' Wilson*), Salome Jens (*Nora Marcus*), John Randolph (*Arthur Hamilton*), Will Geer (*Old Man*)

Plot

New York banking executive Arthur Hamilton has everything a man could want: impressive wealth, a proper wife, a grown daughter married to a doctor. But none of it has brought him fulfilment, and the ageing Arthur fears that he will die before he has truly lived. So, when an old friend from college phones to tell him that he can begin again with a new life, Arthur takes the chance. After signing a contract with the Company, Arthur's death is faked and he undergoes extensive surgery to be 'reborn' as a younger man, Antiochus ('Tony') Wilson, the bohemian painter Arthur has always wanted to be. Relocated to Malibu, California, Tony is attracted to Nora, a free-spirited young woman he meets on the beach, and she gets him to drop his inhibitions and join in orgiastic revelry at a grape-stomping festival. But afterwards, at a cocktail party with his Malibu neighbours, Tony drinks too much and begins to speak about his past as Arthur. His swinging neighbours suddenly take on a seriously threatening demeanour, and Tony discovers to his horror that they are all 'reborns' like him and that Nora is a kind of femme fatale: masquerading as the woman of his dreams, she actually works for the Company. Tony returns to New York to see his wife, who thinks that Tony is a friend of her late husband. She reveals that she understood how unfulfilled her husband had felt but that he had never let her help him. Tony then goes back to the Company. They promise him another surgical attempt at a new life, but after strapping him to a gurney and wheeling him into the operating room, they take his life by boring into his head with a cranial drill. (His dead body will now allow someone else to fake a death and be 'reborn'.)

Comments

Why wasn't Arthur's first attempt to be 'reborn' a success? We get a hint early on when Arthur visits the locations that 'front' for the Company: a clothes-pressing shop (like the old-age wrinkles they will press out of Arthur's face) and a meat-packing plant (like his body which they will carve up). Arthur cannot achieve an emotional or spiritual rebirth through the purely material means of surgery. Another hint comes when the Old Man who owns the Company has to coax Arthur into signing the contract by getting him to completely discount his present life. If Arthur finds no fulfilment in his job, his wife or his family, it is because he sees all these as merely the external trappings of material success and does not look more deeply into them to find meaning (his wife's love, for example). In signing away his present life to the Old Man, Arthur is like Faust selling his soul to the Devil. Finally, with his new life as Tony in California, he merely finds another kind of materialistic striving as he joins others who are desperate for young flesh, who try to recapture their youth through orgiastic drinking and sex. Realising his mistake in the end, Arthur laments: 'The years I've spent trying to get all the things I was told were important, that I was told to want. Things! Not people or meaning, just things. California was the same. They made the same decisions for me all over again, and they were the same things really.'

Seconds can also be read as dramatising the psychological conflict within a closeted gay man (like Rock Hudson) who has been passing as straight but who feels the call of homosexual desires. Arthur's conformist life, which includes marriage to a proper wife, has been rewarded with material success, and yet something is missing. He feels no passion. Then, out of the blue (like a wish-fulfilment fantasy), Arthur receives a phone call from a college buddy, Charlie, who refers to the doubles tennis games they used to play and the trophy they won (they etched '*fidelis eternis*' on the bottom). Later, in the Company waiting room, Arthur – who has been surgically rejuvenated as young Tony – sees another young man giving him meaningful looks, as if 'cruising' him. This man turns out to be the similarly rejuvenated Charlie. It is Charlie who leads Arthur away from his staid married past and towards an emotionally and physically expressive life as a free man in California. There he meets other bohemians like the one who says that she and her group 'change sex'. (In fact, what she actually says is that they 'change sects', but that's not how Arthur/Tony hears it.) Could his homosexuality be the reason why his relationship with Nora fails? Is this why, even after supposedly finding happiness with her, he drinks so heavily at the cocktail party and has a breakdown? By all accounts, Rock Hudson was himself drunk and broke down while playing Tony in this scene. According to Salome Jens (who played Nora), 'Having to cover his homosexuality all the time must have been very hard on him… Lies are the one thing we can't handle. And he was lying. And it drove him nuts. He was an alcoholic, too, and couldn't stop… Rock could not stop after one drink, and that was the way he handled his pain.'[52]

Factoid

Director John Frankenheimer had originally wanted one actor to play both the ageing Arthur and his younger version, Tony, but Rock Hudson refused to act in the film if he had to play the part of the older man.

Blue Steel (1990)

Directed by: Kathryn Bigelow
Written by: Kathryn Bigelow and Eric Red
Produced by: Edward R Pressman and Oliver Stone
Edited by: Lee Percy
Cinematography: Amir Mokri
Cast: Jamie Lee Curtis (*Megan Turner*), Ron Silver (*Eugene Hunt*), Clancy Brown (*Nick Mann*), Elizabeth Pena (*Tracy Perez*)

Plot

Megan Turner is a rookie cop in New York City. She shoots an armed robber at a grocery store, but the perp's gun is secretly stolen by a witness, Eugene Hunt, and so Megan is suspected of having killed an unarmed man. Eugene begins shooting random New Yorkers with the stolen gun, using bullets with Megan's name etched on them and causing her to become a suspect in this serial killer's crimes. Eugene, a wealthy Wall Street type, puts on a Prince Charming façade and begins to court Megan, who initially falls for him. When she discovers who he really is, she has no evidence and he is released. Eugene makes a threatening visit to the home of her mother and father and kills her best friend Tracy. Only kindly Detective Nick Mann believes Megan about Eugene, but when she and Nick become lovers, Eugene shoots him and rapes her. Afterwards, Megan and Eugene engage in a protracted shootout and, when he runs out of bullets, she shoots him dead.

Comments

Blue Steel is a film by a female director about a female cop. Just as Megan is constantly asked why she would want to join the police force and carry a gun, so Kathryn Bigelow has had to answer questions about why she would want to be a director of violent, action-oriented pictures. Bigelow's answer is revealing: 'I find B-movies [such as film noirs] inspiring because they delve into a darkness and talk about the demons that exist in all of us.'[53] Megan's battle with Eugene is a confrontation with her own dark side. Both characters are attracted to the killing power of the gun. The film begins with gleaming close-ups of a gun's blue steel, emphasising its phallic hardness and the sensual insertion of bullets into its chamber. (Bigelow employed a special technique called Innovision, allowing us to see from inside the gun's barrel as the bullets slide in.[54] Even the sound effects in this gun-barrel scene seem erotic: 'the hollow sound of tunnelled air is an aural hard-on: internalised, fluid-driven, raging.'[55]) We then see Megan buttoning up her police uniform over a lacy bra, encasing her femininity within another kind of 'blue steel' as though she herself were becoming a weapon. The robber Megan shoots *is* pointing a gun, but she fires multiple bullets into his body in what is surely an instance of overkill. We find out that one reason Megan became a cop is to overcome the powerlessness of being a passive witness to male violence, such as her father's beating of her mother. Now Megan wields the gun: is she tempted to use excessive force as an overcompensation for her previous weakness? Is she acting in the name of justice or revenge? Eugene is first excited by her when he witnesses her shooting the robber and later, during sexual foreplay, he puts her gun to his head and desires her to shoot. 'We are two halves of one person, you and I,' he tells her, for he represents the killer she could become if she gave way to her dark demons. Yet, when the darkness of male violence surrounds her, how can she defend herself without accessing some of this darkness within? Her father beats her mother. Megan takes him away in handcuffs, but when compassion for him leads her to bring him back home, Eugene is there in her father's chair, as if forgiving her father had only allowed male monstrousness to grow in power. Megan wants to be a wife and mother like her friend Tracy, but this option only seems like a way to become a victim when Tracy is murdered by Eugene. Megan wants romance with a caring lover, but the Eugene who seemed to be her Prince Charming is 'replaced' by a marauding monster, much as the gentle Nick Mann is replaced in her bed by the rapist Eugene. After the rape, Megan refuses just to lie there in the hospital like a victim. It is hard not to cheer as she knocks out a male guard, puts on his uniform and does battle with Eugene gun-to-gun in a lengthy shootout, which ends with her triumphant and him dead. But before Megan kills him, he has run out of bullets and no longer poses her any immediate threat. She shoots him anyway, multiple times. The look in his eye indicates that he *desires* her to shoot him: she has become that absolute symbol of power he loves, that power he felt when he was shooting defenceless people as a heartless killer. In overcoming Eugene's violence, Megan brings out her own.

Suture (1993)

Directed by: Scott McGehee and David Siegel
Written by: Scott McGehee and David Siegel
Produced by: Scott McGehee and David Siegel
Edited by: Lauren Zuckerman
Cinematography: Greg Gardiner
Cast: Dennis Haysbert (*Clay Arlington*), Mel Harris (*Dr Renee Descartes*), Sab Shimono (*Dr Max Shinoda*), Dina Merrill (*Alice Jameson*), Michael Harris (*Vincent Towers*), David Graf (*Lt Weismann*)

Plot

Despite the fact that Vincent is rich and white and Clay is working class and black, they are brothers and everyone sees them as identical twins. Vincent has murdered their father and, in order to evade capture for the crime, he tries to fake his own death by dressing Clay in his clothes, switching their driver's licences and blowing up his own car while Clay is driving. However, Clay survives, although his face has been obliterated and his mind is suffering from amnesia. While psychiatrist Dr Max Shinoda tries to help him reconstruct his memory, plastic surgeon Dr Renee Descartes works on reconstructing his face, using photos and videotapes of Vincent as the model. In the meantime, the police also hound him, suspecting him in the murder of his father and subjecting him to a line-up. But when the witness can't quite identify him, he is freed and effectively cleared of the crime. Once this happens, the real Vincent returns and attempts to kill Clay and take back his own identity and wealth. As the two come face to face, Vincent is a white man wearing black clothes and Clay is a black man dressed in white. As Vincent fires his gun at Clay, Clay shoots back, blowing Vincent's face off. In the end, even though Clay seems to have remembered who he really is, he decides to live the rest of his life as Vincent, marrying Renee and enjoying Vincent's wealthy lifestyle.

Comments

Early in the film, Vincent tells Clay, 'I am a very wealthy man, with expensive things all around me, and I am forced to protect what's mine against people who might feed off my privilege, feed off what doesn't belong to them.' Vincent denies kinship for the sake of wealth. Even though he and Clay (like all men) are really brothers under the skin (despite their colour difference), he tries to kill his own brother just as he has murdered his own father – for money. In an interesting comment on Vincent's soulless greed and paranoia, the all-white building where he lives – a circular structure girded by linked V's of steel – is actually an empty bank. By all accounts, Vincent's father Arthur Towers was himself a predatory capitalist and so, in killing to take his place, Vincent in a sense takes on his father's identity, becoming a Towers, a member of the white patriarchy. It could be said that Clay does the same in the end when he kills Vincent and then lives the rest of his life feeding off Vincent's wealth and privilege. Clay *looks* happy in the photos of him marrying Renee, going to garden parties and playing golf, but is this merely picture perfect, a surface appearance? According to Dr Shinoda, even if Clay 'is able to achieve happiness, it will be false, empty. For he has buried the wrong life, the wrong past, buried his soul.' And yet, although Clay seems to have been sutured into the identity of a wealthy white patriarch, he appears to be a different man from Vincent or their father. Even as the plastic surgeon Renee is moulding his 'Graeco-Roman nose' and 'thin, smooth lips' after Vincent's, the African-American Clay is actually exhibiting the character traits that are supposed to go with these facial features. It is Clay, not Vincent, who has an 'affectionate, kind-hearted gentleness', and Renee falls in love with Clay as she would never have fallen for cruel, anti-social Vincent. It could be that when Clay takes Vincent's place in the end, he will subtly subvert rather than merely repeating him. He might remake the patriarchy in the image of something better.

Devil in a Blue Dress (1995)

Directed by: Carl Franklin
Written by: Carl Franklin, from the novel by Walter Mosley
Produced by: Jesse Beaton and Gary Goetzman
Edited by: Carol Kravetz
Cinematography: Tak Fujimoto
Cast: Denzel Washington (*Ezekiel 'Easy' Rawlins*), Tom Sizemore (*DeWitt Albright*), Jennifer Beals (*Daphne Monet*), Don Cheadle (*Mouse Alexander*)

Plot

Ezekiel ('Easy') Rawlins is an African-American in racially segregated 1948 Los Angeles. Discriminatorily fired from his job and needing money to pay the mortgage on his house, Easy lets himself be hired by white gangster Albright to find a white woman named Daphne who has been frequenting the black part of town. In exchange for information on Daphne but also to satisfy his own desires, Easy has sex with his best friend's girl, Coretta, who is later found murdered, causing suspicion to fall on Easy. This novice private eye eventually clears his name and solves the case of the missing woman. Daphne's fiancé Carter and a man named Terell are rival politicians running for mayor of LA. Terell has threatened to reveal that Daphne is of mixed racial ancestry, thus jeopardising Carter's political ambitions and Daphne's marital hopes. In reaction, Daphne has been trying to obtain incriminating photographs that show Terell to be a paedophile. Daphne tries to seduce Easy to get these photographs, but he resists. In the end, Daphne is kidnapped and almost tortured by Albright (who is working for Terell to get the photos back), but Easy, aided by his violent friend Mouse, saves her in a shootout with Albright and his henchmen.

Comments

By giving Daphne a social history, *Devil in a Blue Dress* complicates her as a femme fatale. At first Easy sees her as a white woman exerting her racial superiority over him as a black man, and she does try to seduce him with her Barbara Stanwyck hair, long fingernails and cigarette smoke. But all of this turns out to be a mere front, for she is really part black and desperately trying to counter a blackmailer in order to save her future marriage. Of course, in hiding the fact of her mixed-race status, she is lying and deceptive like a femme fatale and, when she reveals this truth to Easy, she talks 'like a sinner who wanted to confess'. But who wouldn't lie if telling the truth meant that she couldn't marry the man she loves? Which is the greater sin, the lie she tells in the name of true love or the interracial relationship (hers with Carter or the one between her parents that produced her) which is only a sin in the eyes of a racist society? Daphne is a femme fatale in the sense that white men like Albright project their own fears of women and blacks onto her, saying 'Which part of you is nigger?' as he is about to rape her with a hot poker.

As for this film's private eye, Easy, he can be seen as an upstanding hero. If he hadn't been unjustly fired by his white employer, Easy would not have been so desperate for money as to let himself be hired by white gangster Albright. Despite being beaten by white gangsters and white detectives, Easy avoids committing violence whenever he can and tries to check his friend Mouse's more brutal excesses. Easy also resists Daphne's seductive advances (unlike in the book, where he gives in), and Easy eventually saves her from being assaulted by Albright. But to make a hero out of Easy in this way would be to turn him into a much less interesting character than he actually is in the film. Easy doesn't surrender to Daphne, but it's clear that he wants to. He does succumb to having sex with his best friend's girl Coretta while the man is sleeping in the next room. Was Easy's need (for sex or info) so strong as to justify this act? Coretta is found murdered the next morning. No, Easy didn't do it, and yet he is still in some way implicated; he is not guilt-free. Later, Easy is having an 'innocent' conversation with a white girl, for which he is threatened with retaliation by a racist white boy. Suddenly, the gangster Albright appears and almost forces the white boy to 'suck [Easy's] peter'. Here Albright seems to act out Easy's vengeful wish. In a scene where Easy is being beaten up by Frank (Daphne's brother), Easy's friend Mouse suddenly appears to subdue Frank and torture him, and later, after Easy finds out that his old friend Joppy was the one who betrayed him, it is Mouse who strangles the man. As Mouse says to Easy, 'If you ain't wanted him killed, why you leave him with me?' Director Carl Franklin has described Mouse as Easy's 'alter ego', 'the person that Easy could become but had somehow managed, through all of this, to avoid' – someone 'so cynical', 'so unaware of who he is morally, so comfortable with his place in immorality'.[56] But Mouse can also be seen as Easy's alibi, the person he gets to do his dirty work so that Easy does not have to recognise his own implication in and responsibility for violence. Easy sends Mouse away in the end, but he still thinks of him as a 'friend'. Will he appear again the next time Easy needs to be dissociated from his own immorality?

Factoid

Franklin was originally hesitant to cast Jennifer Beals in the role of Daphne because he feared that Beals's looks (the actress is herself biracial) would tip off viewers right away to the fact of Daphne's mixed-race ancestry, but he was so impressed by Beals's abilities as a performer that he went ahead and cast her anyway.

Bound (1996)

Directed by: The Wachowski Brothers (Andy and Larry Wachowski)
Written by: The Wachowski Brothers
Produced by: Andrew Lazar and Stuart Boros
Edited by: Zach Staenberg
Cinematography: Bill Pope
Cast: Jennifer Tilly (*Violet*), Gina Gershon (*Corky*), Joe Pantoliano (*Caesar*)

Plot

We open on a woman lying bound and gagged on the floor. A flashback reveals that this is Corky, a butch lesbian who has fallen for Violet, who convinced her to help steal two million dollars from Violet's gangster boyfriend, Caesar, a money launderer for the mob. Is Corky like the heterosexual male dupe of traditional film noir who is seduced into crime by a femme fatale and then betrayed? Is it because of her love ties to Violet that Corky ends up bound and gagged? No, it turns out that Caesar is the one who tied up Corky and, in a neo-noir twist on the conventional plot, Violet remains true to Corky, her partner in crime. In the end, Corky escapes from her binding; Violet shoots

Caesar; and she and Corky get away with murder, taking the mob money with them to start a new life together.

Comments

According to directors Andy and Larry Wachowski, this film is not a two-character study but a 'triangle' in which Caesar is as important as Violet and Corky.[57] Again and again, Caesar's low opinion of women leads him to treat them as slaves and then to underestimate their ability to retaliate against his mistreatment. When Caesar first catches Violet alone with Corky, his jealousy turns to mocking contempt: he can't imagine Violet being attracted to a woman when she has such a virile man as himself. Later, he is easily fooled by Violet into believing that a rival male mobster took his money, for he considers her too stupid to have pulled off such a scam. Finally, he continues his domineering behaviour towards Violet even when she has the gun, for he is sure that he knows her to be a weak woman who won't shoot. But Violet does shoot, and she *is* having an affair with Corky, with whom she has successfully executed the robbery. There is thus a sense in which Caesar, by his constant demeaning of women, has brought on his own demise. Hence the irony in having the macho Tom Jones song 'She's a Lady' sung over the closing credits: 'Talkin' about the little lady, and the lady is mine.'

Audiences tend to cheer in the end when, both dressed in black leather jackets and dark sunglasses, Corky and Violet kiss each other (perfectly doubled in female solidarity) and drive off together. They are freely 'bound' to each other, not forced to belong to any man. However, it is possible to see some moral ambiguity in the actions they have taken. Earlier on, Violet has told Corky, 'You made certain choices in your life that you paid for. You said you made them because you were good at something and it was easy. Do you think you're the only one that's good at something?... We make our own choices, and we pay our own prices. I think we're more alike than you want to admit.' In the past, Corky stole and served a five-year jail sentence for it. Violet had sex with men for money, and her 'sentence' has been to serve as Caesar's mistress and slave for five years. Each woman took the 'easy' way to survival: for the butch Corky this was stealing, and for the more 'feminine' Violet it was whoring, and each has paid the price of being 'bound' against her will – being kept in jail or serving as a 'kept' woman. Now they both want out. But look at what they do to get out: Violet uses her seductive feminine wiles against Caesar (whoring), and Corky grabs the briefcase full of money (stealing). In their plot against Caesar, don't they once again choose to take the easy way? And will there really be no price to pay?

Factoid

One sign of the secret affinity between the women is that Violet recognises Corky's arm tattoo as a labrys. Originally associated with the Amazons and with matriarchal societies and since adopted as a symbol by feminists and lesbians, the labrys is a double-bladed axe that can be used for harvests – or as a weapon.

NEO-NOIR INTERNATIONAL

The Samurai (Le Samouraï) (1967)

Directed by: Jean-Pierre Melville
Written by: Jean-Pierre Melville and Georges Pellegrin, from the novel *The Ronin* by Joan McLeod
Produced by: Raymond Borderie and Eugène Lépicier
Edited by: Monique Bonnot and Yo Maurette
Cinematography: Henri Decaë
Cast: Alain Delon (*Jef Costello*), François Périer (*Superintendent*), Nathalie Delon (*Jane Lagrange*), Cathy Rosier (*Valérie, the pianist*)

Plot

Hitman Jef Costello goes to his girlfriend Jane's to establish an alibi. He then carries out a contract by shooting a nightclub owner, but Jef is seen by a female pianist (Valérie) as he is making his exit. However, at the police line-up, Valérie does not identify Jef as the killer, and this, combined with Jane's support of his alibi, gets him released. Jef goes to collect payment, but is almost killed by a henchman working for the mob boss (Olivier Rey) who first hired Jef and who now fears that Jef, after his arrest, is working with the police. Jef beats up the henchman for information, then tracks down and kills the mob boss Rey, who has double-crossed him. Before his death, Rey has contracted with Jef for another hit, this one on Valérie. Jef goes to the nightclub, aims his gun at Valérie, but is shot by police, who then discover that Jef had emptied his gun of bullets before entering the club. In pointing his gun at Valérie, Jef knew he was committing suicide.

Comments

Jef's icy precision as an assassin is the epitome of cool, but the film also presents it as pathological. When Jef dons his trench coat and fedora in front of the mirror, running his fingers meticulously over the hat brim, he solidifies the image of himself as a pro – armoured, frozen-faced, impenetrable. Yet this very image, which allows Jef to escape notice as he pulls his coat collar up around his neck and walks with his head down so that his hat brim hides his face, also threatens to bury him as a man. Is there any human being left inside these killer's clothes? Jef is anonymous to the point of losing any sense of self, lying so silent and still in his apartment that he seems one with his inanimate surroundings. Director Jean-Pierre Melville replaced the colour labels on cigarette packs and water bottles with black-and-white photocopies of same to show the drabness of a world experienced by a man who won't allow himself to feel, and the film's overall blue-grey colour scheme was designed to match Jef's eyes, as if seen from his half-dead perspective. The ritual repetitions of Jef's work, as when he methodically tries key after key after key until one fits the ignition of the car he is stealing, are also obsessive attempts to avoid losing control and becoming distracted by the life around him, like the girl in the next car who is trying to flirt with him. Melville presents Jef as a 'schizophrenic', torn between life and death, between opening himself up to love and remaining 'impassive, because nothing can deflect him from his mission' as a hitman.[58] In the shot where we first see Jef in his apartment, Melville uses a stop-and-go track-back combined with a zoom-forward to dramatise Jef's 'schizophrenia', the life-and-death conflict within him.[59] In the end, although Jef allows himself to fall in love with Valérie, he can only find enough feeling within him to deviate slightly from the narrow path of death he has followed for so long. He returns to the scene of the first crime and points his gun at Valérie as he had at the club owner, repeating the same explanation as to why: 'I was paid to.' Only this time, because Jef cannot shoot Valérie, he has brought an empty gun and he lets himself be killed instead of her. It is better to have died of love than to continue his empty life as one of the walking dead.

Clean Slate (Coup de torchon) (1981)

Directed by: Bertrand Tavernier
Written by: Jean Aurenche and Bertrand Tavernier, from the novel *Pop. 1280* by Jim Thompson
Produced by: Adolphe Viezzi and Henri Lassa
Edited by: Armand Psenny
Cinematography: Pierre-William Glenn
Cast: Philippe Noiret (*Lucien Cordier*), Isabelle Huppert (*Rose*), Jean-Pierre Marielle (*Le Péron and his brother*), Stéphane Audran (*Huguette Cordier*), Eddy Mitchell (*Nono*), Guy Marchand (*Marcel Chavasson*), Irène Skobline (*Anne, the teacher*)

Plot

Lucien Cordier is a police chief in 1938 French colonial Africa. He lets his wife Huguette have a live-in lover, Nono, without challenging her cover story that the man is her brother. Cordier himself has a mistress (Rose), but he does not stop her husband from beating her up in public. Cordier lets two pimps taunt him and literally push him over onto the ground, and he allows his police superior Marcel to boot him in the behind. All around him, Cordier sees racist whites take advantage of their colonial position to exploit the indigenous blacks, but he does virtually nothing. Cordier appears to be an utter wretch – lazy, weak and ineffectual. Yet things are not what they seem. Cordier shoots the two pimps and then protects himself from prosecution by having the blame fall on Marcel if his police superior ever comes after him for the crimes. Cordier shoots Rose's abusive husband, who was also a sadistic racist, and then lets people believe that a black servant and the husband killed each other. Cordier teaches Rose how to shoot a gun, then takes money out of the house where he lives with his wife and her lover. When Huguette and Nono go to Rose's house and threaten her for the money, she shoots them both. Directly or indirectly, Cordier has rid the town of some bad people, and he has gotten away with it. And yet, near the end of the film, he tells the one woman (Anne) with true compassion for him that she mustn't love him. 'I'm all alone,' he says, and 'I've been dead for such a long time.'

Comments

At the start of the film, Cordier builds a fire to help warm some African boys exposed to the cold of a solar eclipse. But by the end of the film, when he sees a black boy suffering in the heat of the sun, Cordier points his gun at him, then points the gun at himself and finally droops his head in despair. Cordier has moved from believing that small, compassionate acts can help, to fearing that all he can really do to alleviate the suffering of others and himself is to wipe everyone out. (A closer translation of the title, *Coup de torchon*, would be 'clean sweep'.)

The film initially sets up a *Death Wish* kind of scenario in which, after watching Cordier be repeatedly humiliated and take no action in the face of evil, we cheer him on as he definitively vanquishes his oppressors and saves others from further predation. The pimps are exploiting women, and Marcel also exploits women by seeing underage prostitutes, so there seems to be a certain justice in destroying the pimps and pinning their murder on Marcel. Similarly, Rose's husband is abusive towards her and blacks, so the world won't miss him when Cordier rubs him out. Note, though, that Cordier's executions are not exactly disinterested: he gets revenge against the pimps and Marcel for having humiliated him and, with Rose's husband gone, Cordier now has unimpeded access to her for sex. The fact is that the 'impartial justice' Cordier dispenses is more and more corrupted by a very personal self-interest. The clearest example of this is when Cordier kills the black servant whose only 'crime' is that he knows about the murder of Rose's husband and might inform on Cordier. Cordier kills him even though this man seems to be good. Director Bertrand Tavernier remembers the bewildered reaction that audiences had to this killing, with two viewers saying, 'My God, how can we accept the fact that [Cordier] killed the black guy. It's impossible.'[60] Cordier may think he is visiting divine judgement upon sinners ('God told me to kill them'), but he is horribly, tragically confused about the difference between right and wrong action, about whether he himself is a force for good or evil.

Consider his scenes with the pimps. Cordier catches them shooting at African corpses floating in the water, as if the bodies were trash and not, as Cordier explains, 'entrusted to the river' as part of a burial ceremony. But Cordier accepts a bribe not to arrest the pimps for breaking the law, and he allows them to make him take a shot at the corpses himself. Cordier's compassion for the others who suffer becomes a kind of self-serving complicity with their victimisers. The pimps then shove him into the river, as if he were one of the African corpses, 'shot' by white men. For Cordier, the only alternative to this uncomfortable oneness with the defeated dead is to rise up against the oppressors, as he does when he later shoots the pimps and rolls *them* into the river. Here Cordier destroys the evil pimps but only *by identifying with them as aggressors*, using violence in their place. Yet, after killing them, Cordier sinks to the ground and lies there as if dead. A part of him realises that, in shooting them, he has killed himself, committing immoral acts in the name of morality. This is why, even in the midst of his self-righteousness, Cordier knows his soul is dead. Rather than fighting injustice, his violence has increasingly made him one of the oppressors, damning everyone to destruction.

The Element of Crime (Forbrydelsens element) (1984)

Directed by: Lars von Trier
Written by: Lars von Trier and Niels Vørsel
Produced by: Per Holst
Edited by: Tómas Gislason
Cinematography: Tom Elling
Cast: Michael Elphick (*Fisher*), Esmond Knight (*Osborne*), Meme Lai (*Kim*), Jerold Wells (*Kramer*), Ahmed El Shenawi (*Therapist*), Lars von Trier (*Schmuck of Ages*)

Plot

Fisher is undergoing hypnotherapy in Cairo. The psychiatrist enables Fisher to access his memory of the time when he was a police detective in Europe, trying to solve a sex/murder case in which a serial killer is suffocating and cutting up girls who sell lottery tickets. To catch the killer, Fisher adopts the method outlined by his old police mentor, Osborne, in a book called *The Element of Crime*, whereby the detective immerses himself in the same environment and identifies as closely as possible with the murderer, who is known as Harry Grey. Fisher retraces Grey's steps from town to town, checks into hotels under Grey's name and even has an affair with a woman (Kim) he thinks was Grey's mistress. Fisher believes he has discovered a pattern to Grey's murder sites and that, in order to complete the pattern (which forms the letter 'H'), Grey will commit his last killing in the town of Halle. Using a girl as bait, Fisher waits for the killer to strike, but when a Horse's-Head figurine (left by the killer at a murder site and picked up by the detective) falls from Fisher's pocket, the girl becomes frightened of Fisher himself and screams. Fisher suffocates her in the process of holding her to quiet her down and thus becomes her murderer. However, police chief Kramer tells Fisher that Osborne has confessed to two of the killings and then hanged himself. It would seem that Osborne had followed his own detection method of identifying with the killer and had taken it too far, and now Fisher has done the same thing – the detective becoming the very murderer he had sought to stop.

Comments

The European environment in which Fisher immerses himself is a post-apocalyptic world of perpetual rain, decay and darkness. Plunging into this world enables Fisher to share the killer's experiences, but it also adversely affects him in the way that it did the killer, causing splitting headaches and a split in his personality that turns him towards the dark side. Fisher is like this film's skinhead divers who jump from great heights hoping that the ropes around their ankles will break their falls before they drown in the water below. Fisher takes a similar risk, plunging into the killer's environment to understand what shaped his disturbed mind in the hope of stopping him before that same disturbance begins to take over Fisher himself. Even if Fisher's near-suicidal method fails, it is still better than Kramer's homicidal approach, which is simply to shoot everyone who might be a threat. At one point, Kramer even shoots at the sister of one of the murdered lotto girls!

In the world of decay and dissolution surrounding him, Fisher holds on to his method in an attempt to understand the madness, but he holds on so tightly that the method itself becomes a kind of madness. Fisher tries to comprehend and contain Grey's path of destruction by seeing the murder sites as forming an 'H', a pattern which is 'systematic to the last detail' and which Fisher must follow 'according to the book. I can't stop now.' But what Fisher doesn't realise is that the pattern he sees may be self-projected, a sign that he has overinvested in the murders to the point of duplicating them himself. This film might be a critique by director Lars von Trier of his own tendency towards hyper-organisation, for at this point in his career the 'rigorous storyboarding and the meticulous planning of every shot in advance was symptomatic of von Trier's almost maniacal desire to control every last detail'.[61]

Hypnotherapy in Cairo also fails to give Fisher a narrative pattern he can cling to for stability, since Cairo is almost submerged by sand much as Europe is under water. Von Trier has pointed out that, while the psychiatrist is 'only interested in the lead that Fisher has to follow', the monkey on the psychiatrist's shoulder is 'immensely interested in his own sexual organ – he sits there and plays with it quite violently'.[62] Thus, while Fisher thinks that he is gaining control of and through his mind, his body is doing some terrible things. He has rough sex with Kim from behind as she is thrown over the hood of a car; he slaps her around in bed much as Grey may have done with his mistress; and Fisher eventually kills a little girl, completing the pattern of Grey's sex/murders. At the end, Fisher shines a flashlight down a storm drain and sees the blinking eyes of a nocturnal rodent. Despite his search for enlightenment ('I want to wake up now. Are you there? You can wake me up now.'), Fisher has found only the darkness and corruption within himself.

Fireworks (Hana-Bi) (1997)

Directed by: Takeshi Kitano
Written by: Takeshi Kitano
Produced by: Masayuki Mori, Yasushi Tsuge and Takio Yoshida
Edited by: Takeshi Kitano and Yoshinori Oota
Cinematography: Hideo Yamamoto
Cast: Takeshi Kitano (*Yoshitaka Nishi*), Kayoko Kishimoto (*Nishi's wife*), Ren Osugi (*Horibe*), Susumu Terajima (*Nakamura*)

Plot

Police detective Nishi leaves a stakeout to visit his dying wife in a nearby hospital and, while he is gone, his partner Horibe is wounded by the gunman they had under surveillance. When Nishi returns to the scene, he tackles the gunman to the floor but is then knocked aside. This leaves other policemen (Nakamura and Tanaka) to pile on the gunman, but he shoots them from below, wounding Nakamura and killing Tanaka. Nishi shoots the gunman in the head and then continues firing all his remaining bullets into the corpse. Forced to resign from the police force, Nishi borrows money from a yakuza loan shark in order to support Tanaka's widow and to buy painting supplies for Horibe, who is now confined to a wheelchair and needs a reason to live. When Nishi runs out of funds, he robs a bank, continuing to give to Tanaka's widow and Horibe but also using the money to take his dying wife on a trip that retraces the places they visited on their honeymoon. Nishi is now being trailed by both cops and criminals: the yakuza who want repayment of their loan, and Detective Nakamura who wants Nishi for the bank robbery. Nishi shoots all the yakuza, then asks Nakamura if he can have a few more moments with his wife. Nakamura grants the request and then hears two shots ring out: Nishi and his wife have died in a suicide pact.

Comments

As noted in the press kit for this film, *Hana-Bi* (the Japanese word for fireworks) is composed of two parts: '*Hana* (flower) is the symbol of life while *Bi* (fire) represents gunfire, and so death.' It is possible to read the film as a contrast between Horibe, who learns to live again by painting flowers where the faces of brute animals would normally be, and Nishi, who uses the brute violence of gunfire to kill others and eventually to take the lives of his wife and himself. But it is also possible to understand the film in the exact opposite way, and viewers may be surprised to hear that director Takeshi Kitano favours this reading. According to him, Horibe 'starts painting to forget about his loss; it's his way of seeking oblivion. On the other hand, Nishi realises the importance of his wife and friend and starts taking responsibility for them... To me, by dying, Nishi and his wife take a step forward to the next life, while Horibe, by not killing himself, will not be able to live a fruitful life. By choosing to live he chooses to die slowly, a slow suicide.'[63]

I would like to propose a third reading, one that sees a *similarity* between Horibe and Nishi, a connection between painting and violence – like the hyphen connecting *Hana* (flower) and *Bi* (fire) in *Hana-Bi* – rather than a contrast. Just as painting saves Horibe from despair, so violence becomes a form of art for Nishi, a means of confronting and surviving his terrible situation. The connection here can be seen in Kitano's own life where, after a terrible motorbike accident left half of his face scarred and partially paralysed, he turned to painting in the hospital as a way to recovery. Horibe's paintings in the film are actually Kitano's, but of course the violence in the film was also 'painted' or directed by Kitano. Creating scenes of gunfire and other 'fireworks' is Kitano's art form in this film called *Hana-Bi* or *Fireworks*, and Kitano himself plays Nishi, a man of lethal violence. When Nishi's dying wife attempts to water some wilted flowers in a vase by the sea, an obnoxious man yells at her that it's pointless. Nishi intervenes, punching and kicking the man into the sea where he holds him under water until blood blossoms around the man's head (an aestheticisation of violence). While Horibe is starting to paint, Nishi is using a chopstick as his paintbrush to poke out a gangster's eye and paint the floor red or spray-painting a taxi to use it as a fake police car in the bank holdup, which we will watch from an 'aesthetic' distance on black-and-white surveillance monitors. As Horibe uses white and yellow to include the Japanese words for snow and light in one of his paintings, Nishi uses yellow blasts of gunfire to kill the yakuza in their white car in the snow, a scene viewed from a painterly distance in a high overhead shot. Finally, after Horibe paints the Japanese word for suicide in red, this stands in for the blood we don't see when Nishi and his wife fulfil their suicide pact. Instead, the camera shows the two of them embracing and then cranes up and pans over to the ocean. We hear two shots, but their actual death is omitted. It is as if their life together has continued on into nature and the afterlife. As Kitano has said, 'In *Hana-Bi* I wanted to rearrange the violent scenes as much as I could, using omissions or the distance of the camera or the duration of time. If one pursues the beauty of formality to its ultimate point, it can lead to the Kabuki form.'[64] Whatever one thinks of its morality, violence is the art by which Nishi attempts to survive and do good for others in this life and to take himself and his wife into the next.

Amores Perros (2000)

Directed by: Alejandro González Iñárritu
Written by: Guillermo Arriaga Jordán
Produced by: Alejandro González Iñárritu
Edited by: Alejandro González Iñárritu, Luis Carballar and Fernando Pérez Unda
Cinematography: Rodrigo Prieto
Cast: Emilio Echevarría (*El Chivo*), Gael García Bernal (*Octavio*), Goya Toledo (*Valeria*), Alvaro Guerrero (*Daniel*), Vanessa Bauche (*Susana*)

Plot

A car crash at a Mexico City traffic light marks the intersection of three stories about characters from different walks of life: 1. Before the collision, working-class Octavio enters his Rottweiler (Cofi) in dogfights to win enough money to run away with Susana, the wife of his abusive brother Ramiro. 2. Fashion model Valeria has the perfect life – a successful ad campaign, a new apartment, a handsome lover – until the car crash leaves her with a terrible leg injury. Then, in trying to retrieve her white poodle (Richi) from a hole in the apartment's floorboards, she further damages her leg, which has to be amputated. 3. After the crash, the dog Cofi is rescued and nursed back to health by El Chivo, a man who has taken in and loved many stray dogs. When he comes home one day to discover that

Cofi has killed all his other dogs, El Chivo, who is a hitman, almost shoots Cofi but chooses instead to give up the way of the gun.

Comments

El Chivo began as an idealistic college professor in a country controlled by a right-wing dictatorship. The only way he could see to make the world better for his family was to turn to violence, but the terrorist bombings he engaged in merely landed him in jail for 20 years. Since his release, he has succumbed to nihilism and despair, becoming a hitman for hire. But just when El Chivo is following his latest human target, the car crash occurs behind him. Isn't there already enough senseless violence in the world without his deliberately adding to it? By taking in stray dogs, El Chivo is already showing some impulse towards saving himself, and his rescue of Cofi continues this self-healing trend. El Chivo's biggest challenge comes when, after being nursed back to health, Cofi kills all his other beloved dogs. But rather than give in to further destruction and despair by shooting Cofi, El Chivo spares the dog and keeps him around as a constant reminder of the killer he himself once was and must keep from becoming again. By continuing to love Cofi (whom he has renamed 'Blackie'), El Chivo acknowledges his own dark deeds but believes in the possibility of his own redemption. ('Blackie' is also the nickname of the film's director, Alejandro González Iñárritu.) At the end of the film, El Chivo and Blackie cast themselves out from society into a black desert on the outskirts of Mexico City. It is here that El Chivo will do penance for his sins until he is worthy of returning to rejoin the daughter he left behind so long ago. It is his memory of her that has kept alive some faith in his own goodness. ('We are also what we have lost' are the words that appear at the end as part of director González Iñárritu's dedication: 'My wife and I lost a child, our boy, who was called Luciano, when he was two days old. I dedicated *Amores Perros* to him.')[65]

Before his self-exile, El Chivo devises an unusual alternative to carrying out his last hit. He brings both Luis (his current target) and Gustavo (the man who ordered the hit) to the same location. These two men are rivals in business and possibly rivals in love, but they are also, as El Chivo reminds them, half-brothers. El Chivo refuses to be the paid intermediary making it easy for one to kill the other through him. Instead, if one man is going to deny brotherhood and commit murder, he'll have to do it face to face, as Cain slew Abel. Releasing each man from the handcuffs that had bound him to a separate post, El Chivo suggests that the two men talk out their differences, but he also gives them the option of going for the gun he leaves between them, of lunging at each other like wild dogs. It is their choice.

Ichi the Killer (Koroshiya 1) (2001)

Directed by: Takashi Miike
Written by: Sakichi Satô, from the comic by Hideo Yamamoto
Produced by: Dai Miyazaki and Akiko Funatsu
Edited by: Yasushi Shimamura
Cinematography: Hideo Yamamoto
Cast: Tadanobu Asano (*Kakihara*), Nao Omori (*Ichi*), Shinya Tsukamoto (*Jijii*), Alien Sun (*Karen*)

Plot

When yakuza boss Anjo disappears and is feared dead, his lieutenant Kakihara tortures a series of suspects to gain information. To take the most notorious example, one man is suspended from chains with hooks stuck through the skin of his back and then has boiling oil poured over the wounds. When Kakihara is accused of having gone too far in his interrogations, he enthusiastically cuts off his own tongue as self-punishment. The sadistic Kakihara, it turns out, is also quite a masochist. His boss Anjo used to give him the most pleasurable pain and now Kakihara is looking for a suitable substitute. When bargirl

Karen enjoys sadistically stretching a suspect's cheek, Kakihara thinks he may have found his ideal partner, but the punches she then throws at Kakihara's face are just too weak. Another contender's fist smashes into Kakihara's mouth but only ends up gnawed to the bone. Meanwhile, as Kakihara continues his investigation into Anjo's disappearance, he keeps finding the sliced-up bodies of fellow gang members, and all the evidence points to a man named Ichi. Is Ichi the ultimate punisher of evil and the answer to Kakihara's masochistic dreams? Ichi, in his black-leather, muscle-padded suit with a yellow #1 on the back, may seem like a superhero, and in one scene he rescues a prostitute (Sara) from being raped and beaten by her pimp. Ichi uses a blade which pops out of his boot to split the pimp's face and torso in half. But then Ichi himself tries to assault Sara and, when she fights back, kills her with his blade! Not only is Ichi morally confused regarding women, but his 'good guy' attacks on evil men turn out to have been programmed by a mastermind named Jijii, who hypnotised Ichi to kill others, not for the sake of good, but as part of a revenge plot. Ichi's personality swings between unhealthy extremes: either he is a weeping wimp who can't fight back or he is a sadistic psychopath who explodes into indiscriminate violence. In their final confrontation on a rooftop, Kakihara imagines that Ichi slices his forehead with the blade and causes him to plunge to an orgasmic death. In actual fact, Ichi just lies there crying on the rooftop, being kicked by a small boy whose father Ichi had killed.

Comments

As Ichi remembers it, when he was young he once witnessed a schoolgirl being raped by bullies. It could be argued that the trauma of this event divided Ichi into a kind of split personality: one who feels the girl's pain and wants to rescue her, and another who identifies with the bullies and desires to rape her. (Thus, in slicing the pimp in half, Ichi repeats his own splitting.) One side of Ichi defeats the bullying pimp in order to save Sara, but Ichi's other side then moves to assault her and ends up killing her with his blade. So, this blade which pops out of Ichi's boot is not just a knife he uses against bullies. It is also a kind of erection which appears when Ichi grows excited by violence, and the film makes it clear that the only way Ichi can climax is when he kills. Kakihara too has been traumatised into confusing sex with suffering. His facial scars and piercings are signs of the masochistic 'enjoyment' he received from boss Anjo's abuse. Kakihara's traumatic experiences have left him brutalised and unhinged: at the end of the film, his torn mouth – which he normally uses pins to keep closed – drops open like the jaws of a savage beast. Interestingly, Kakihara's masochistic tendencies can be compared to those of female rape victims. Karen says that, after being raped, 'I wanted a sadist… to carve me up with the blade' and 'I wanted to die, to fall into despair.' This is also what Kakihara wants. He claims to find pleasure in pain, but his true desire is death because self-annihilation is the only way he can now imagine to end the abuse: 'I really want to lose myself in desperation.' And so Kakihara imagines that Ichi is the ultimate sadist whose blade penetrates Kakihara's forehead – a violation that finally takes him into the void. In reality, Kakihara's traumatised mind has at last gone completely mad.

demonlover (2002)

Directed by: Olivier Assayas
Written by: Olivier Assayas
Produced by: Xavier Giannoli
Edited by: Luc Barnier
Cinematography: Denis Lenoir
Cast: Connie Nielsen (*Diane de Monx*), Charles Berling (*Hervé Le Millinec*), Chloë Sevigny (*Elise Lipsky*), Dominique Reymond (*Karen*), Jean-Baptiste Malartre (*Henri-Pierre Volf*), Gina Gershon (*Elaine Si Gibril*)

Plot

The Paris-based Volf Corporation is negotiating to buy distribution rights to Japanese Internet anime porn in which female action figures fight each other and are raped by tentacled demons. Diane has her superior, Karen, drugged and kidnapped in order to take over her power position at the negotiation table. Diane is a spy working for Mangatronics, which wants to gain control of the product and shut out rival company Demonlover, represented by Elaine. Diane sneaks into Elaine's hotel room in order to steal some computer files and, when surprised by Elaine, ends up in a fight to the death with her in which Elaine is killed. Blackout. When Diane regains consciousness, she finds herself demoted to a position below Elise, a woman who used to be her inferior in the company hierarchy. Elise, a spy for Demonlover, is blackmailing Diane with a video that shows her killing Elaine. And Hervé, Diane's co-worker with whom she had enjoyed flirtatious power games, also turns out to be a spy for Demonlover. When he rapes her, she shoots him in the head. Elise then takes Diane to a country chateau in which she is imprisoned and forced to submit to sexual humiliation and torture – all to suit the fantasies of a teenage Internet customer who pays for the vicarious pleasure of exerting his power over her.

Comments

In the beginning, Diane thinks she is the rising star and winning competitor in her real world of corporate power games. What she doesn't realise is that the game is playing her. Sooner or later a new female action figure (Elise) will take Diane's place in the power hierarchy just as Diane replaced Karen. And Diane will go from being the attacker ('I was raped,' Karen says about Diane's takeover) to being a victim: Hervé rapes Diane and then she is assaulted on video for a teenage boy to watch. Diane's real world gradually merges with the 'reel' world of violent porn videos, as she comes to realise that the excitement of screwing the competition – and the horror of getting screwed – are really the same in both worlds. As writer/director Olivier Assayas has said, 'I do believe that today's obsession with sado-masochistic sexuality is to do with the power games within the corporate system, which find a distorted mirror in S&M.'[66] In the film's opening scene on board the corporate jet with its cold white decor, Diane may appear calm and in complete control ('a real ice queen') as she uses a syringe to drug Karen's Evian water, but what Diane is doing is really extremely violent and driven by a wild desire for dominance. Fiery explosions on the plane's video monitors tell the truth about Diane's destructive act, and later, in an ironic turn, Diane's own car will crash and burn as she tries to escape her tormentors (but they recapture her and take her back to the chateau for more televised torture). More and more often throughout the film, we see Diane reflected in glass surfaces as she is increasingly drawn into the realm of violent video porn. The last we see of her is her image on a computer monitor showing an interactive sexual torture site, for she has finally been completely absorbed into the corporate world of dominance and submission.

Oldboy (2003)

Directed by: Chan-wook Park
Written by: Jo-yun Hwang, Chun-hyeong Lim and Chan-wook Park, from the comic by Garon Tsuchiya and Nobuaki Minegishi
Produced by: Dong-ju Kim
Edited by: Sang-Beom Kim
Cinematography: Jeong-hun Jeong
Cast: Min-sik Choi (*Dae-su Oh*), Ji-Tae Yu (*Woo-jin Lee*), Hye-jeong Kang (*Mi-do*), Dae-han Ji (*No Joo-hwan*), Dal-su Oh (*Park Cheol-woong*)

Plot

Suddenly and for no apparent reason, ordinary businessman Dae-su Oh is kidnapped and imprisoned for 15 years, then just as inexplicably released. Hungry for revenge, Dae-su eats a *live* octopus at a sushi bar. He falls for and eventually sleeps with a beautiful young sushi chef, Mi-do, who helps him locate the place where he was kept confined. There Dae-su tortures the prison manager for further information by prying out the man's teeth with the claw end of a hammer and, when a horde of prison guards attacks, Dae-su savagely beats them off with the hammer (in a brutally extended fight scene shot entirely in one take). The mastermind of it all, Woo-jin Lee, gives Dae-su five more days to solve the mystery of what has been happening to him or Mi-do will be killed. Eventually, Dae-su is able to remember that, back in high school, he saw Woo-jin having sex with a girl and made a careless comment about it afterwards, which grew into a rumour that apparently led the girl to kill herself. This girl also turns out to have been Woo-jin's sister. Woo-jin has taken revenge against Dae-su by locking him up until Dae-su's daughter has come of age and by hypnotising the two into falling in love with each other: Mi-do is Dae-su's daughter. Dae-su now cuts off his own tongue to punish himself for having started the rumour about Woo-jin's sister and to beg Woo-jin not to tell Mi-do about the father-daughter incest. Woo-jin commits suicide. Dae-su has himself hypnotised to forget that Mi-do is his daughter and reunites with her in the end.

Comments

In the course of this film, Dae-su changes from an ordinary businessman (whom we first see comically drunk) into a superhero-fighter, able to defeat an entire corridor full of attackers with a single hammer. However, director Chan-wook Park does not film Dae-su's violence in a way that gets us to glory in his heroic vengeance. Rather, the violence is shown as 'brutal, repetitive, maybe a bit boring', which 'underlines how meaningless the fighting is'.[67] Dae-su becomes not an angelic avenger but (as he calls himself) a 'monster' and a 'beast', devouring a live octopus in the same way he threatens to eat Woo-jin's body parts. Dae-su turns into the mirror image of Woo-jin: both come to realise that, once they've had their revenge, the pain it was designed to dull returns with full force. Vengeance cannot make up for what they have lost.

Equally important is the realisation that revenge cannot repress the truth for long. As Chan-wook Park notes, 'The vengeance represented is merely the transferring of a guilty conscience by people who refuse to take the blame themselves.'[68] Woo-jin blames the rumour-starting Dae-su for the death of his sister, but it was Woo-jin himself who had an incestuous relationship with her and thus contributed to her suicidal sense of shame. And Dae-su must understand that he too is susceptible to the same kind of 'beastly' incestuous desire. Not only did he look on voyeuristically as Woo-jin had sex with his sister back in high school, but Dae-su falls for his own daughter Mi-do. Dae-su's father-daughter incest thus mirrors Woo-jin's brother-sister incest, and both men are thus complex characters with angelic and beastly sides. (A split-screen shot shows one half of Woo-jin's face paired with the other half of Dae-su's.) In the end, by repressing knowledge of the fact that Mi-do is his daughter, Dae-su tries to 'split into two people': the 'monster' side that knows about the incest will die, leaving the other side to be happy as her blissfully ignorant lover. But when Dae-su embraces Mi-do at the end, his smile gives way to crying as the angel in him seems to remember that he is also a beast.

Bad Education (La Mala Educación) (2004)

Directed by: Pedro Almodóvar
Written by: Pedro Almodóvar
Produced by: Agustín and Pedro Almodóvar
Edited by: José Salcedo
Cinematography: José Luis Alcaine
Cast: Gael García Bernal (*Angel/Juan/Zahara*), Fele Martínez (*Enrique Goded*), Daniel Giménez Cacho (*Padre Manolo*), Lluís Homar (*Sr Manuel Berenguer*)

Plot

In 1980, film director Enrique receives a visit from a man claiming to be his childhood friend Ignacio, who has brought him a story to film.

The story tells of how, back in 1964, the two friends fell in love while at a Catholic boys' school, but Father Manolo, a paedophile priest, abused Ignacio and jealously expelled Enrique from the school. The story continues: now it is 1977, and Ignacio, who has become a pre-op transsexual, visits Manolo and blackmails him, threatening to make the priest's abuse public if he does not pay for Ignacio's sex change. We leave the story and return to real life in 1980. While planning to make a movie of the story, film director Enrique functions as a 'private detective' and discovers that the man who brought him the story is very like that 'classic film noir character – the femme fatale'.[69] This man, who deceptively claimed to be the grown-up Ignacio in order to seduce Enrique into giving him the 'Ignacio' role in the film, is really Ignacio's younger brother Juan, who does not love Enrique. Even worse, it was Juan who actually conspired with Manolo to kill Ignacio. Ignacio had been blackmailing Manolo and stealing the limelight (as a drag artiste) and the money (for drama school) from younger brother Juan, an impoverished actor.

Comments

Juan may be deceptive, seductive and fatal, but he is a multidimensional character with complex motives. After killing his brother, Juan takes his place, as if he could atone for the murder of Ignacio by being at one with him, by becoming him. (Both Ignacio and Juan are played by the same actor, Gael García Bernal.) Ignacio had wanted to become a woman before he was killed, and Juan satisfies this wish by acting the 'Ignacio' role of a transsexual drag queen in Enrique's film. When they were young, Ignacio had desired Enrique before Father Manolo separated them, and 16 years later Juan fulfils this desire by sleeping with Enrique. Ignacio had sought revenge on Father Manolo for having sexually overpowered him as a boy, and years later Juan turns the tables on Manolo, seducing and abandoning the older man. Juan, who claims to be Ignacio but who insists on being called by the name of 'Angel', is suffering from an identity crisis in which he is halfway between Juan and Ignacio, an avenging angel who is out to punish those who have done wrong to Ignacio – a group of sinners which includes Juan himself. When Juan plays the part of Ignacio in the film and acts out a scene where he is murdered by priests who do not want the sexual abuse revealed, it as though Juan is re-enacting his own murder of Ignacio, only this time Juan has taken his brother's place, perhaps as a way of punishing himself for the murder he committed.

Lust, Caution (Se, jie) (2007)

Directed by: Ang Lee
Written by: Wang Hui Ling and James Schamus, from the story by Eileen Chang
Produced by: Bill Kong, Ang Lee and James Schamus
Edited by: Tim Squyres
Cinematography: Rodrigo Pieto
Cast: Tony Leung Chiu-Wai (*Mr Yee*), Tang Wei (*Wong Chia Chi/Mak Tai Tai*), Joan Chen (*Yee Tai Tai*), Leehom Wang (*Kuang Yu Min*), Tou Chung Hua (*Old Wu*)

Plot

Hong Kong, 1938. After her success in a patriotic school play, university student Wong Chia Chi takes on an even more challenging role as a spy working for the resistance (of Chinese against Japanese). Her femme-fatale mission is to seduce Mr Yee, a collaborationist official, and to lure him to his assassination. After a failed first attempt (he is too cautious and untrusting to let himself be trapped), Wong tries again several years later in Shanghai, but at the last minute she changes her mind and warns Yee, enabling his escape. Yee's response is to have all the members of the resistance group rounded up and shot dead – including Wong.

Comments

Wong's decision to save Yee leads to her own death and that of her resistance comrades. Why does she do it? Translator Julia Lovell gives one possible explanation when she refers to Wong as a 'gullible', 'self-deceived heroine' and to her decision as an 'impulsive abandonment of the cause for an illusory love'.[70] Certainly, Wong begins as something of a naïve schoolgirl, but it seems too simple to describe her in the end as a foolish romantic who is merely mistaken in thinking that she and Yee share a kind of love. In order to seduce Yee, Wong has to act as though she loves him. While some would say that she foolishly forgets she is acting, screenwriter James Schamus argues that Wong '"becomes herself" only when she takes on the identity of another, for only behind the mask of the character... can [Wong] truly desire, and thus truly live – playacting allows her to discover her one real love'.[71]

When Wong first starts acting in patriotic plays, she is able to break out of the restrictive gender role she is expected to play in life (the demure and recessive woman) and express her passion, which mingles with a dawning sexual desire for Kuang, the drama group's leader. But Kuang, though he shares that desire, won't *act* on it. Despite longing glances in Wong's direction, Kuang channels all his passion into politics – and also into violence, as when he stabs Tsao, a man Kuang considers to be a traitor to the cause. So, in 'performing' as a seductive spy in her 'scenes' with Yee, Wong discovers and expresses her own active sexuality, as revealed in the film's physically graphic sexual encounters between the two. At first Yee rips open Wong's clothes, ties her hands behind her back and takes her brutally from behind. For him, sex is an extension of the torture he is used to inflicting on prisoners. But then, after Wong intuits how lonely Yee's cruelty has made him, the two have sex face to face and she tries to calm his violent thrusting and move him towards tender embracing, at which point they both seem to experience pleasure together. Later, when Yee gives Wong a secret message to deliver, she assumes it is political and part of his manoeuvring for greater power, but instead it turns out to be an order for a diamond ring. When Yee then trusts Wong enough to go with her to the jeweller's and when he is moved to see how happy the ring makes her, Wong has reason to believe that, at this moment, Yee has put his passion for her above politics. Her act of seduction has paradoxically led to a true expression of his love for her – and then of her love for him, when she saves him from assassination. Yee subsequently betrays her, but does this mean that she was wrong to have placed her faith in love? Without this faith, will there ever be any chance of a different ending?

NEO-NOIR REMAKES

The Postman Always Rings Twice (1946)

Directed by: Tay Garnett
Written by: Harry Ruskin and Niven Busch, from the novel by James M Cain
Produced by: Carey Wilson
Edited by: George White
Cinematography: Sidney Wagner
Cast: Lana Turner (*Cora Smith*), John Garfield (*Frank Chambers*), Cecil Kellaway (*Nick Smith*)

The Postman Always Rings Twice (1981)

Directed by: Bob Rafelson
Written by: David Mamet, from the novel by James M Cain
Produced by: Charles Mulvehill and Bob Rafelson
Edited by: Graeme Clifford
Cinematography: Sven Nykvist
Cast: Jack Nicholson (*Frank Chambers*), Jessica Lange (*Cora Papadakis*), John Colicos (*Nick Papadakis*)

Plot

Depression-era California. Nick owns a roadside diner and gas station. When drifter Frank comes passing through, Nick offers him a job as a mechanic and handyman. At first, Frank refuses, but when he sees Nick's young wife Cora, he changes his mind. Frank and

Cora fall for each other and plot to murder her husband and make it look like a bathtub accident. When this first attempt fails, they try again, staging another 'accident' by killing Nick with a blow to the head and then sending him in his car over a cliff. Unfortunately, the car gets stuck part way down, and in attempting to dislodge it, Frank doesn't get out fast enough and ends up plunging downwards too. While recovering in a hospital, Frank yields to pressure from the district attorney to sign a complaint against Cora for attempted murder, and she, feeling betrayed, then dictates a confession implicating Frank along with herself in the death of her husband. But it turns out that the man who took the confession was working for the clever defence attorney, who proceeds to get both Cora and Frank off. The two return to working together in the diner, but they must fight the mutual distrust that has grown between them. By uniting forces, they defeat a blackmail attempt from the man who took Cora's confession, and Cora even forgives Frank for the brief affair he has with another woman. In the end, just as the two seem to have recovered their love and are planning to settle down as a family (Cora is pregnant), Frank swerves to avoid an oncoming car, and Cora dies in the accident. The 1981 remake ends here. In the original 1946 film, Frank is then sentenced to death for having murdered Cora for her money. Ironically, he is now convicted of a killing he didn't do, whereas before he had escaped punishment for a murder he actually committed.

Comments

The Postman Always Rings Twice is sometimes mentioned in the same breath with *Double Indemnity* as another quintessential film noir in which a femme fatale seduces and manipulates another man into killing her husband for money, after which she betrays the poor sap and eventually drags him down to destruction with her. However, *Postman* is considerably more complicated and interesting than that. The most memorable scene in the 1946 Lana Turner-John Garfield version is the one where Frank first meets Cora. A tube of lipstick rolls across the diner floor, and as Frank looks to see where it came from, his eyes rise to view a bare-legged beauty framed in a doorway, dressed in white hot pants, a revealing blouse and a white turban. This sizzlingly exotic sight attracts Frank's attention, but she looks not at him but at herself in her compact mirror, holding out her hand for the lipstick. When he makes her come to him to get it, she looks annoyed but also intrigued, posing for him in the doorway for a moment while applying her lipstick before closing the door on him. It is possible to read Cora here as a seductive tease playing hard to get, yet she can also be viewed more sympathetically, as a woman with ambivalent feelings. Later she tells Frank that she married Nick to gain protection from all the younger men who were merely lusting after her. But while she has found some security in having an older husband (he bought her those clothes, for example), she feels no passion for him. Her white-hot clothes are thus a semi-conscious 'MAN WANTED' sign, for she wants love (both passion *and* security), while her haughty body language shows her fear that Frank may be just another lustful male trying to take advantage of her. Cora believes in fidelity, and it is only when Nick won't dance or swim (or make passionate love) with her that she allows Frank to do so.

As far as Cora's being a femme fatale who manipulates Frank into killing her husband, it is more likely that they share the responsibility for this plot. Frank has a solemn face when, thinking aloud, he first suggests the idea ('I'd like to see him… drive off a cliff'), but Cora convinces them both that he was only joking. Later, when she proposes the plan in all seriousness and he protests that, before, he had merely said it in jest, she is right to claim that he had already 'started to think about it a little'. They are true partners in crime as well as in love. Finally, when it comes to the murder itself, the film does not excuse what Cora (or Frank) does to her husband, but it goes to great lengths to explain it. Rather than kill, Cora and Frank first attempt to run away together, but no one will pick them up when they are hitchhiking, and a passing car knocks Cora into a dirty roadside ditch, so she returns to the diner. Some have seen her as a haughty bitch who can't stand having her white clothes sullied, but the scene can also be read symbolically: is Cora so wrong to be afraid of being dirt poor during the Depression? Then there is the fact that Nick treats her like a domestic slave, bragging that he can dirty his own clothes because he has her there to wash them for free. And when Nick decides for both of them that they will move to arctic Canada where Cora will care for his paralysed sister, we can read Cora's horror as indicating her uncaring attitude and her lack of wifely devotion, or we can understand her desperate need to escape the paralysis of her own cold marriage to an unloving husband. When Cora dies in the car accident at the end, her hand drops the same tube of lipstick that had been the sign of her semi-conscious need for Frank when they first met, but he cannot help her now. No 'femme fatale' ever died with such pathos.

The 1981 Jack Nicholson-Jessica Lange version is notorious for being more explicit in its sex scenes, owing to the lifting of Production Code censorship restrictions. Best remembered is the scene early on where Frank grabs Cora and she shouts in fury, fighting him off. However, when he forces her up against a kitchen counter and kisses her, she seems to respond but then backs away from him – yet with a smile on her face. Then, pinned against a cupboard, she tries to push him away, but when he goes down on her, she begins to writhe in pleasure. When he lays her down on the kitchen table, she pushes him off, but this is only so that she can sweep the flour and baked bread off the table (along with a bread knife that she could have used against him) to clear a place for them to have sex. 'All right, come on!' she says, pulling his hand to her crotch, undoing his belt, and eventually getting on top of him and riding him to orgasm. Because this scene shows Cora responding sexually to being forced, it is open to criticism for implying that women want to be raped. Screenwriter David Mamet has explained that Cora feels 'anesthetise[d]' in her marriage to her older husband and that Frank comes along as a 'younger, more virile stranger' to bring her 'violence, sexuality, regeneration'.[72] While it may be that Frank's violence provides Cora with some shock therapy, re-awakening her passion along with her ambition for a better life, this very violence also seems to taint the love between Frank and Cora, contaminating it with sadomasochistic and murderous desires. In a later scene, Cora leaves her husband upstairs and comes coquettishly down to the kitchen to see Frank, but as she is bent over giving milk to the cat, he suddenly punches her in the rear end and grabs her from behind, which she protests she doesn't like. However, when he then becomes more tender and starts kissing the back of her neck, she bites his hand and turns around to laugh in his face. Cruelty and domination have become an integral part of their lovemaking. This fact is most disturbingly apparent in the scene where they kill Nick, run his car off a cliff and must make it look as though they were roughed up in the 'accident'. Hellishly lit by the car's red taillights, Cora hits Frank across the face with a bottle and gets turned on. 'Hurt me!' she says, and after he tears at her clothes and knocks her to the ground, she lies down in the grass, her hand between her legs pointing the way, and Frank proceeds to take her right there, so close to the body of her dead husband. For Cora and Frank, sex has become inextricably entangled with death.

Factoid

Actress Jessica Lange said, 'What I liked about Cora is that her character isn't clear-cut. I don't think you can just see her as a victim of the two men, her husband and her lover; she victimises them too. I think she's more a victim of the time and of her own limitations.'[73]

Purple Noon (Plein soleil) (1960)

Directed by: René Clément
Written by: René Clément and Paul Gégauff, from the novel *The Talented Mr. Ripley* by Patricia Highsmith
Produced by: Raymond and Robert Hakim
Edited by: Françoise Javet
Cinematography: Henri Decaë
Cast: Alain Delon (*Tom Ripley*), Maurice Ronet (*Philippe Greenleaf*), Marie Laforêt (*Marge Duval*), Bill Kearns (*Freddy Miles*)

Plot

Philippe Greenleaf is a rich American playboy leading a hedonistic life abroad. (Yes, his name is Philippe and he speaks French even while vacationing in Italy, but never mind: this is a French-made film.) Philippe's father, a wealthy industrialist, dispatches Tom Ripley to find Philippe and bring the wastrel son back home to the US where he is expected to shape up and assume a responsible position in the family business. Tom hangs around Philippe in Italy, burning with envy of his moneyed lifestyle and feeling excluded whenever Philippe gets together with girlfriend Marge. One day aboard Philippe's yacht, Tom stabs his friend to death and takes on his identity, forging his signature on bank checks, wearing his clothes and checking into hotels under his assumed name. When Freddy, one of Philippe's friends, makes an unexpected visit and catches on to the impersonation, Tom kills him. He then fixes things so that the police will suspect that Philippe murdered Freddy and then killed himself, leaving behind a will that bequeaths his riches to Marge. In the process of 'consoling' Marge, Tom (now appearing as himself) seduces her, thus acquiring both Philippe's woman and his wealth. In the film's last scene, he is sipping a cool drink under an umbrella on a sunny beach, savouring his moment of absolute triumph. Too bad the police have just discovered Philippe's corpse tangled up in the yacht's anchor rope, incriminating Tom. As the film ends, the police have Tom called away from his sunny beach scene (he walks out of frame), leaving a picture-perfect view from which he is once again excluded.

Comments

One of the key characteristics marking *Purple Noon* as a *neo*-noir is its elaborate gay subtext, though this has not been noted nearly as often as the more overt homoerotics in the Anthony Minghella version. If you know Quentin Tarantino's extended riff on the gay subtext of *Top Gun* (as seen in the film *Sleep with Me*), you have to wonder what he would say about *Purple Noon*. Early on, Philippe and Tom pick up a girl together and they both start kissing and fondling her while she sits between them in a carriage. It is as though they are making physical contact with each other through her. Philippe walks around with a cane, pretending to be blind, and also says that he's blindly in love with Marge – but is he only pretending? Later, as Philippe makes out with Marge on a couch, Tom takes his friend's clothes from his closet and puts them on, then speaks in Philippe's voice to a mirror, kissing his reflection while saying, 'My little Marge knows I love her and that I won't go with that nasty Tom to San Francisco.' Here Tom pictures himself as Philippe making love to Marge, but he also imagines Philippe kissing *him*, or himself lip to lip with Philippe. The choice between marrying Marge and going with Tom to San Francisco becomes a choice between hetero- and homosexuality. When the threesome are on the yacht, Marge receives Philippe's attentions in the cabin below while a shirtless Tom sits alone and frustrated above deck with the knobby handle of the steering wheel between his legs. Then, when Philippe is lying on top of Marge on the deck, Tom is lying on his back several feet from them in the same one-leg-up position as Marge, as if he wanted to occupy her place under Philippe. In a later scene where it is just the two men left on the boat, Tom looks down when Philippe tells him, 'I love Marge.' Soon after that, Tom uses a knife he has concealed near his swim trunks to stab Philippe. A violent penetration becomes the closest approximation to a sexual one, and Tom merges his identity with Philippe, deciding that to be him is the only way to have him. Tom then checks in and out of hotels with/as 'Philippe', as though the crime he's hiding is homosexuality as well as murder. In killing Freddy, Tom eliminates another man who had been a rival for Philippe's affections, and in seducing Marge he can imagine himself being bedded by Philippe in her stead. It's no wonder that, the last we see of Tom, he is sprawled in a beach chair with his shirt open to reveal a naked torso and his swim trunks bulging. He is living an erotic dream – until the rude awakening when he is arrested.

Factoid

Anthony Minghella (director of the remake) believed that there was a problem with the original version, *Purple Noon* – actor Alain Delon was just too gorgeously handsome to play Tom Ripley: 'It's very hard to imagine him ever wanting to be anybody else, particularly as everybody who watched the film wanted to be him.'[74]

The Talented Mr. Ripley (1999)

Directed by: Anthony Minghella
Written by: Anthony Minghella, from the novel by Patricia Highsmith
Produced by: William Horberg and Tom Sternberg
Edited by: Walter Murch
Cinematography: John Seale
Cast: Matt Damon (*Tom Ripley*), Gwyneth Paltrow (*Marge Sherwood*), Jude Law (*Dickie Greenleaf*), Cate Blanchett (*Meredith Logue*), Philip Seymour Hoffman (*Freddie Miles*), Jack Davenport (*Peter Smith-Kingsley*)

Plot

Wealthy American dilettante Dickie Greenleaf is idling away his time in Italy, so his disapproving father sends penniless Tom Ripley abroad to bring the prodigal son home. But Tom falls for Dickie and his glamorous lifestyle, vicariously enjoying the clothes and cars that come with being a member of the leisured class. When one of Dickie's casual affairs results in the pregnancy and suicide of a local girl, Tom covers up for his friend, but Dickie decides that Tom is getting too close for comfort. When the two of them are out on the bay in a motorboat, Dickie attempts to gain some distance from Tom by calling him a 'bore' and a 'leech'. Unable to listen to his friend giving voice to Tom's own worst fears about himself, Tom strikes Dickie with the boat's oar. An enraged Dickie throws himself at Tom, trying to strangle him, and Tom then kills Dickie with the oar in what could be seen as self-defence. Tom now assumes his dead friend's identity, forging Dickie's signature on banknotes to get the money to buy fancy clothes, attend the opera and fill an apartment with classy furnishings that would otherwise be beyond his means. When Freddie, one of Dickie's expatriate friends, arrives unexpectedly and spots the imposture, Tom has to kill him in order to avoid being exposed as a fake. Unfortunately for Tom, 'Dickie' then becomes a suspect in Freddie's murder, so Tom must end his impersonation, which he cleverly does by typing a suicide note from 'Dickie' in which he confesses to the murder and praises Tom as a friend. Although Dickie's fiancée Marge suspects that Tom killed Dickie, Dickie's own father believes Tom and rewards him with considerable wealth for having been a loyal friend. Then, just as Tom seems embarked on the dream life he has always desired, including a shipboard romance with another man (Peter), he has a chance encounter with a woman who knew him as 'Dickie', and Peter overhears her call Tom by that name. In the end, rather than confess to Peter and hope for forgiveness, Tom strangles his new love so that his masquerade and murder of Dickie will not be revealed. Technically, Tom gets away with murder, but he is profoundly lost and alone.

Comments

According to director Anthony Minghella, Tom is not just some psychopath totally unlike you or me. Instead, he is 'representative of the circumstances that many people find themselves in. Every message we get from the print media and from the electronic media is to try and discover ways to change ourselves, that who we are and what we have is not enough, that we require transforming.'[75] In a class-conscious society, the penniless Tom feels unworthy and incomplete, so he identifies with an image of wholeness, with Dickie, the golden boy whom everyone admires. During the opening credits, we see Tom reflected in the shards of a broken mirror, as if he were struggling with a fragmented and unfinished sense of self. Then, when he first spies Dickie's bronzed body and godlike good looks through binoculars, Tom says, 'This is my face.' Soon, after becoming Dickie's friend, Tom is imitating his voice and trying on his clothes in a full-length standing mirror. When Dickie enters the room, Tom runs behind the mirror, with his head visible above it and Dickie's body reflected in it, as though the two could be combined into one image of perfection. However, in attempting to acquire another's wholeness, Tom actually becomes profoundly alienated from himself. First, Dickie may be admired because he is handsome and has money, but he is narcissistic and cruel, using others only for his own benefit. Tom may want to admire himself-as-Dickie in the glass, but what he needs to realise is that this idealised image of his friend is actually hollow: 'It's all about class; it's all about smashing the window and getting into the world of privilege, and what a folly it is and what an empty room we discover it is.'[76] Second, since wholeness is a myth (nobody is perfect), Tom condemns himself to an endlessly frustrating pursuit when he tries to acquire perfection through another. He will never be able to impersonate the perfect Dickie because nobody can, not even Dickie himself. The ideal that Tom wants to embody will always be beyond him, and he will kill again and again in a foredoomed effort to close the gap between himself and the idealised other. This gap opens when Dickie catches Tom wearing his clothes and sends him out of the room so that Tom is no longer reflected with Dickie in the mirror. Similarly, when Tom leans his head on a sleeping Dickie's shoulder and their two faces (one frontal, the other in profile) are reflected as combined in a train window, Dickie wakes up and forces a separation between them. Even after Tom kills Dickie and assumes his identity, he has still not achieved his ideal, for Freddie sees through Tom's performance and has to be killed to prevent him from exposing the fraud. In one scene where Tom is on a motorbike, he is frightened to see his own reflection replaced by the dead Dickie's, as if his friend had come back from the grave to assert the continuing difference between him and Tom, the lack in Tom that means he will never be his idol. It is fitting, then, that in the last we see of Tom, a mirrored door seems to throw back several broken reflections of him before closing to leave him in darkness. He has not secured his own identity by acquiring that of a rich man. He has only lost himself.

The Manchurian Candidate (1962)

Directed by: John Frankenheimer
Written by: George Axelrod, from the novel by Richard Condon
Produced by: George Axelrod and John Frankenheimer
Edited by: Ferris Webster
Cinematography: Lionel Lindon
Cast: Frank Sinatra (*Major Bennett Marco*), Laurence Harvey (*Raymond Shaw*), Janet Leigh (*Eugenie Rose Chaney*), Angela Lansbury (*Mrs Iselin*), James Gregory (*Senator John Yerkes Iselin*), Khigh Dhiegh (*Dr Yen Lo*)

Plot

Returning from the Korean War, Raymond Shaw is awarded the Congressional Medal of Honour for bravely combating the enemy and for saving his own platoon. Publicly, the members of that platoon support Raymond's version of events, but in private they begin to have disturbing dreams in which Raymond is not the hero but a villain who strangles one of his own men and shoots another through the forehead. Major Ben Marco comes to realise that these nightmares are in fact memories; that the platoon was captured and brainwashed by communists, and that Raymond has been programmed to kill while retaining no memory of his evil deeds. Meanwhile, Raymond's mother, Eleanor Iselin, has been engineering her husband Johnny's rise to power. Johnny is a Joe McCarthy-like senator who preys on people's fears of communist infiltration of the US. Eleanor arranges for Raymond to marry Jocie, the daughter of more liberal Senator Thomas Jordan, in the hope that Jordan will support Johnny's bid for the vice-presidential nomination. But when Jordan vows to block the bid, Eleanor uses the queen of diamonds from the card game of solitaire to trigger Raymond's programming and to compel him to kill Jordan and Jocie. It turns out that right-wing demagogue Eleanor is actually in cahoots with the communists, who are using red-baiting as an elaborate cover to gain Sino-Soviet control of the US government! Eleanor's next command is for Raymond to shoot the presidential nominee at the party's Madison Square Garden convention so that Johnny can take his place and become the next President of the United States. However, what she doesn't realise is that Major Marco has gotten to Raymond first and deprogrammed him by making him conscious of all the terrible things the communists and his mother have made him do. Raymond takes his sniper's perch at the convention, but rather than kill his programmed target, he shoots Johnny and his own mother instead.

Comments

Among the most striking scenes in *The Manchurian Candidate* are the nightmares that cause Major Marco and another soldier to wake up screaming. These dreams begin peacefully enough with the members of the platoon attending a women's garden club meeting where a matronly speaker is discussing hydrangeas, but as the camera turns around the room, the little old ladies seated in the audience are replaced by sneering Russian and Chinese communist officials, and the female speaker is transformed into the sinister Dr Yen Lo, who either physically takes her place or, even more disturbingly, sometimes seems to be speaking his evil words through her mouth. These nice middle-American ladies are a screen memory implanted in the minds of the platoon to cover up the truth about their capture by the communists, but the horrible reality is starting to seep through in the men's dreams. Moreover, the nightmarish image of communist rhetoric coming from the mouth of an arch-conservative American lady will be revealed as the horrible truth when Republican matron Eleanor Iselin is discovered to be the Red Queen, a communist operative who has infiltrated the heartland of America. From Raymond's perspective, xenophobia is compounded by matriphobia (Mommy is a commie!), a fear of foreign influence combining with a suspicion about his own mother's mind control over him. At first Eleanor seems to foster the natural transfer of his affections from her (his mother) to Jocie (his future wife), who attends a costume ball dressed as the queen of diamonds, as if to attract Raymond's attention away from his mother, the Red Queen. But Eleanor turns out to be a horrifically interfering and smothering mother who pulls Raymond into a too-passionate kiss after she gives him the command that leads to his killing of Jocie. Eleanor also debilitates Raymond by removing all the strong father figures from his life, replacing her first husband with hen-pecked stepfather Johnny and ordering Raymond to kill his future father-in-law Jordan.

Raymond's use of violence may appear to be successful in the end: by shooting his domineering mother and his weak-willed stepfather, he foils the communist plot to take over America. But we should not overlook the fact that Raymond then goes on to shoot himself. It is as though, having been overcome by his paranoid fears of both external (foreign) and internal (familial) threats, Raymond makes a desperate attempt to fire back and ends up destroying everyone, including himself. Director John Frankenheimer has said that, with *The Manchurian Candidate*, 'I wanted to do a picture that showed both how ludicrous McCarthy-style far-right politics are and how dangerous the far-left is also, how they were really exactly the same thing, and the idiocy of it all.'[77] Maybe the thing we most have to fear is fear itself and what that fear can make us do.

The Manchurian Candidate (2004)

Directed by: Jonathan Demme
Written by: Daniel Pyne and Dean Georgaris, from the screenplay by George Axelrod and the novel by Richard Condon
Produced by: Tina Sinatra, Scott Rudin, Jonathan Demme and Ilona Herzberg
Edited by: Carol Littleton and Craig McKay
Cinematography: Tak Fujimoto
Cast: Denzel Washington (*Ben Marco*), Meryl Streep (*Eleanor Shaw*), Liev Schreiber (*Raymond Shaw*), Jon Voigt (*Senator Thomas Jordan*), Kimberly Elise (*Rosie*), Jeffrey Wright (*Al Melvin*)

Plot

It wasn't hard for the filmmakers to find a more recent example of war for the film's background. This remake updates the military conflict from the Korean War to the (first) Gulf War. Upon returning home from Kuwait, Raymond Shaw is lauded as a hero and a saviour of his men during Operation Desert Storm. In this version of the film, his mother Eleanor is herself a US Senator and it is her own son Raymond whom she pushes as Vice President. The members of Raymond's platoon lionise him in public but are plagued by nightmares that tell a very different story of what happened in Kuwait. Gradually, Major Marco remembers being captured and brainwashed in a desert island facility by operatives of Manchurian Global, a multinational corporation specialising in defence contracts. Microchips were implanted in the soldiers' brains so that they could be programmed to kill and then forget, but Marco eventually recovers a horrible memory of Raymond suffocating a fellow soldier and of Marco himself shooting another one through the forehead. It turns out that Raymond's mother Eleanor is in league with Manchurian Global, and when a rival senator (Thomas Jordan) threatens to expose her plot and to take her son's place on the party's ticket, she triggers Raymond's programming and has him kill Jordan (and Jordan's daughter Jocelyne, with whom Raymond is in love). Marco makes a heroic effort to alert Raymond to the fact that he is being cruelly used by others to gain power, but, in a shocking turn of events (especially for viewers of the original film version), Marco's intervention has itself been engineered by Manchurian Global, and *his* programming is now activated to get him to shoot the presidential nominee so that Raymond can take the man's place and become Manchurian's puppet President in the White House. However, with the last shred of autonomy and humanity they retain, Raymond and Marco derail the plot by having Marco shoot Raymond himself and his mother. The film ends with Marco making a voluntary return to Manchurian's desert island facility and showing US intelligence what was really done to him and his men there.

Comments

In this film's last image, we see a photograph of Marco together with Raymond and the fellow soldiers in their platoon. As Marco holds the picture under water, ocean waves wash over it, gradually seeming to obliterate the men's faces. This is a film about remembering what actually happens to our soldiers in war rather than covering up the truth with a whitewash of lies and propaganda. As director Jonathan Demme has said, the film ends 'on a disturbing and haunted note' which 'gave us the opportunity to comment on war and what soldiers are forced to do', to comment on 'the exploitation of soldiers – bodies for billions'.[78] The first *Manchurian Candidate* was a satire on rabid right-wing fears of a vast communist conspiracy to take over the US government. By contrast, this film is serious about the danger it sees, about 'what is arguably the biggest threat to humanity today: the multinational corporations who profit from war'.[79] The film opens on Major Marco telling a troop of awestruck boy scouts about Raymond's heroic actions in war, but this is the story Marco has been brainwashed to relate. It is a lie implanted by war profiteers and, in furthering this lie, Marco is unwittingly acting as their agent to recruit more young men for war. For much of the film, as Marco is increasingly plagued by horrible memories of what really happened in war and as he tries to reveal this truth to others, he is viewed as nothing more than a 'crazed vet', a ranting maniac who is sick in the head. But Marco's 'illness' deserves attention, because as a returning veteran he is owed our care and because he has important truths to tell. Although it is the operatives of the multinational corporation who have captured and performed invasive procedures on the men, they are brainwashed into believing that Arabs with strange tattoos caught and tortured them. The soldiers are programmed to see 'foreigners' as the enemy, so that Manchurian Global can have wars to sell their weapons. And anyone who stands in the way of profit is an 'enemy': Raymond drowns the more liberal Senator Jordan, holding his head under water, just as he suffocated one of his own platoon buddies with a plastic bag back at the desert facility – because the corporation told him to, triggering his conditioned response against the 'enemy' with words that make Raymond see a bright white light, obliterating his own humane identity. When Raymond suffocates his brother-in-arms or drowns the Senator's daughter, the woman he loves, he is drowning himself.

Point Blank (1967)

Directed by: John Boorman
Written by: Alexander Jacobs, and David and Rafe Newhouse, from the novel *The Hunter* by Richard Stark (Donald E Westlake)
Produced by: Judd Bernard and Robert Chartoff
Edited by: Henry Berman
Cinematography: Philip H Lathrop
Cast: Lee Marvin (*Walker*), Angie Dickinson (*Chris*), Keenan Wynn (*Yost*), Carroll O'Connor (*Brewster*), Lloyd Bochner (*Frederick Carter*), Michael Strong (*Stegman*), John Vernon (*Mal Reese*), Sharon Acker (*Lynne*), James Sikking (*Hired Gun*)

Plot

After helping to pull off a heist at the abandoned prison of Alcatraz Island in San Francisco, Walker is betrayed by his wife Lynne and his partner Reese. Reese shoots Walker point blank and leaves him for dead in a cell. But Walker survives and, with information from a mysterious man named Yost, tracks the double-crossers to Los Angeles in order to get back his share of the robbery money. He first confronts Lynne, but when she ODs on pills, Walker gets Lynne's lookalike sister, Chris, to seduce Reese while Walker sneaks into the room. The frightened Reese tries to escape and ends up falling from his penthouse roof. Walker then attempts to collect his money from Reese's associates in the mob, following further tips from Yost and going from man to man up the organisation hierarchy in an effort to find someone who will pay him. After two henchmen are shot dead in an ambush meant for Walker, Carter's boss Brewster arranges with mob accountant Fairfax to take Walker back to Alcatraz Island and give him his cash. But when Brewster is killed in a double-cross by Fairfax and when Yost turns out to *be* Fairfax (he has been manipulating Walker all along in order to kill off the competition and make himself head of the organisation), Walker decides in the end not to take the money finally being offered to him. Instead, he merely steps back into the shadows of Alcatraz.

Comments

Point Blank combines American film noir with the European art film (Godard, Antonioni, Melville) to create one of the most stylistically innovative neo-noirs ever made, and in this case style adds considerably to substance. In an early scene, shots of Walker striding down an airport corridor, his shoes click-clacking on the floor, are intercut with shots of Lynne robotically putting on make-up and having her hair done at a beauty salon. Not only does the clanging of his footsteps indicate the inexorability of his vengeful movement towards her, but she seems to be preparing herself for sacrifice to him, as though she were calling out for an end to the emptiness of her consumer lifestyle, the loveless life she has known ever since she betrayed him. And Walker himself seems reduced to nothing but this vengeful movement, to one of the walking dead who lives only to get even with those who wronged him. Chris tells him that he died (emotionally, spiritually) at Alcatraz, and indeed Walker is a kind of ghost haunting the guilty ones who are still living. Walker himself kills no one in this movie. Instead, he is a mere 'catalyst' prompting others to kill themselves (Lynne and Reese) or each other (the men in the mob), bringing the culpable to their own 'self-destruction'.[80] The film indicts a society where gangsters are indistinguishable from businessmen and where corporate greed amasses money and possessions that bring no fulfilment. In this 'white noir', sunny LA is a glass and concrete city of empty materialism, a 'hard', 'cold', and 'sterile' world.[81]

If 'I want my money' Walker is both this greedy world's embodiment and its dead end, he also represents the possibility of renewed love and future hope, as in the scene where he makes love with Chris, exchanging his dark 'avenger' suit for the warm flesh of his naked closeness to her. Innovative editing in this scene takes us from a shot of Walker and Chris to one of Walker and Lynne in bed together, suggesting that he may be able to recapture with Chris the love he had with Lynne. However, this gives way to a cut of *Reese* in bed with Lynne, as Walker remembers her betrayal, and then to a cut of Reese in bed with *Chris*. Although Walker was the one who got Chris to seduce Reese, Walker seems to fear that she will cuckold *him* just as Lynne did. Thus the editing in this scene shows Walker's hope of love battling with his fear of treachery. The ending of the film is similarly (and brilliantly) ambiguous. Does Walker step into the shadows because he has finally achieved his purpose as an avenging ghost and can now be what he has really been all along – a dead man, a man who was killed at Alcatraz? Or does Walker leave the money behind because he has finally learned that his own greed and desire for vengeance have merely made him susceptible to Yost's manipulation and betrayal? Does Walker's disappearance indicate that he is a changed man who can now leave and live a new life with Chris?

Factoid

Director John Boorman has said that Lee Marvin's intense performance as Walker was rooted in the actor's own experience as a young soldier during World War II: 'The young Marvin, wounded and wounding, brave and fearful, was always with him. The guilt at surviving the ambush that wiped out his platoon hung to him all his days... He should have died, had died, in combat... Lee knew how to play a man back from the dead. Superficially seeking revenge, but more profoundly trying to reconnect with life.'[82]

Payback (1999) (Director's Cut, 2006)

Directed by: Brian Helgeland
Written by: Brian Helgeland and Terry Hayes, from the novel *The Hunter* by Richard Stark (Donald E Westlake)
Produced by: Bruce Davey

Edited by: Kevin Stitt
Cinematography: Ericson Core
Cast: Mel Gibson (*Porter*), Gregg Henry (*Val Resnick*), Maria Bello (*Rosie*), David Paymer (*Arthur Stegman*), Deborah Kara Unger (*Mrs Lynn Porter*), William Devane (*Carter*), Lucy Alexis Liu (*Pearl*), James Coburn (*Justin Fairfax*)

Plot

After helping to rob some Chinese gangsters, Porter is betrayed by his wife Lynn and his partner Resnick. Lynn shoots Porter in the back and leaves him for dead. However, Porter survives and tracks down Lynn. He confronts her, but she ODs on heroin. Porter then tries to get his money from his former partner, but when Resnick won't pay and when he threatens to rape Porter's girlfriend Rosie, Porter shoots him. Porter then works his way through a series of Resnick's associates in the Chicago mob, shooting Carter, getting Stegman shot, shooting a hood who insults Rosie, shooting two killers in a urinal and finally shooting a female assassin who tries to ambush him just as he is recovering his money from the mob. In the end, Porter is bleeding from bullet wounds, but we see him smile as Rosie drives the getaway car, enabling him to escape with his money.

Comments

It is probably unfair to be too harsh in one's judgement of *Payback*. First, this was Brian Helgeland's directorial debut. Second, he was fired from the film, which was then subjected to studio-ordered re-shoots (to make it more humorous). Third, by the director's own admission, this was never intended to be more than a straightforward genre film, 'my little tough-guy noir movie. It wasn't reaching for the stars. It's not unusually ambitious'.[83] Yet what is most interesting about *Payback* may be how its relative lack of innovation and complexity make it a lesser film than *Point Blank*. (Still, to be as fair as possible to Helgeland, it is his Director's Cut we will consider here.) In *Payback*, the protagonist is named 'Porter', which, unlike

'Walker', has no symbolic resonance. There is likewise no great 'walking' scene. Porter simply waits outside his unfaithful wife's apartment and then (predictably) surprises her when she comes home. Whereas Walker's presence showed how self-destructive was the mob men's greed, Porter does not convey this complex theme because he simply shoots the men himself. And *if* the killings have a metaphorical meaning, they just show Porter as being caught up in the same macho competitiveness, as when the shooting of the men at the urinal proves that Porter's 'gun' is the biggest. The colour scheme in *Payback* remains a bleak blue-grey, which does not dramatise Porter's struggle to become human again in the way that the gradually warming colours of *Point Blank* (from grey to yellow to red) show Walker's desire for love and hope. And, in the final scene, after shooting virtually everyone, Porter does take the money, and he seems to be rewarded for his violence and greed by being reunited with his girl in the end, who drives him to safety. The immorality of this unequivocally happy ending is a stark contrast to the fascinating ambiguity of Walker's final scene. (Curiously, Helgeland's own view is that Porter dies from his bullet wounds just minutes after the movie ends and thus never gets to live a new life with Rosie, but it seems unlikely – especially given Porter's and Rosie's smiles – that many viewers will see the ending this way.)

Factoid

Helgeland has said that one of the reasons he was fired from the film was that he had included a scene where a dog gets shot – this despite the fact that no harm was done to the actual dog.

Fingers (1978)

Directed by: James Toback
Written by: James Toback
Produced by: George Barrie

Edited by: Robert Lawrence
Cinematography: Michael Chapman
Cast: Harvey Keitel (*Jimmy Fingers*), Tisa Farrow (*Carol*), Jim Brown (*Dreems*), Michael V Gazzo (*Ben*), Marian Seldes (*Ruth*)

Plot

New York City. Jimmy aspires to be a concert pianist like his mother, but his loan-shark father keeps pressing him to collect on the unpaid debts owed by other men. During one collection attempt, Jimmy is arrested for carrying illegal gambling slips and has to spend the night in jail. The next day, he fails his big audition for a piano recital at Carnegie Hall. Jimmy also loses Carol, the woman he loves, when she leaves him for Dreems, a super-macho club owner who treats her as his sexual slave. Meanwhile, Patsy Riccamonza is bragging that he stiffed Jimmy's father on a loan, and the father wants Jimmy to shoot the man if he won't pay up. However, Patsy is a big-time gangster: Jimmy will sleep with the man's girlfriend to punish him, but he refuses to go as far as killing him. Yet when Jimmy finds that his father has had his brains blown out by Patsy's men, Jimmy goes looking for the gangster and, at the conclusion of a brutal fight in a hotel stairwell, shoots him dead.

Comments

The last we see of Jimmy, he is sitting in his apartment naked and utterly desperate, like a little boy lost. He has not found a way to decide between two future paths but instead remains trapped between them, unable to live either one. This is shown by the fact that, in this last image, Jimmy still has one hand on the piano (representing the artistic life he has failed at) while his other hand is on the window overlooking the street (representing the mobster life he doesn't want). Writer/director James Toback refers to the struggle within Jimmy as being between 'the poetic side and the gangster side',[84] and this internal division is even apparent from the clothes that Jimmy wears, which include blue jeans and a leather jacket but also a pink shirt and a fancy white scarf.

Music is Jimmy's ideal world. He carries a boom box with him wherever he goes, even playing 'Summertime, Summertime' in the dead of winter, as if music could enliven the whole world, replacing violent death and discord with harmony. He even sings Bach to stop a fight from breaking out in jail. But music is not strong enough to prevail, as evidenced by Jimmy's mother who has tried to make it as a concert pianist but is now confined to a mental institution. In the same way, brutally masculine forces will work to destroy Jimmy's feminine artistic spirit. Initially, he has some romantic success with Carol, the sculptress he loves. Saying that 'I'm going to bring you into your dreams of yourself', Jimmy does not force himself on her but instead tells her he needs *her* to want him, and when she responds they make love. However, Carol's artistic temperament has been damaged by men who abused her, and she has become a masochist in thrall to a sadistic brute ironically named Dreems. When Jimmy won't dominate her the way Dreems does, she leaves Jimmy, causing him to feel that his sensitivity and compassion make him less of a man.

Similarly, his own father belittles him ('I should have strangled you in your crib') for failing as a gangster, for not standing up and demanding payment from the debtors. In what Jimmy does to Patsy, it is unclear whether Jimmy is taking revenge for his father or *against* him. Is Jimmy trying to prove he is a 'real man' like his father, or is he trying to get back at his father for having destroyed his ideals and his gentle spirit? Patsy and Jimmy's father both have younger girlfriends – women they have in a sense 'stolen' from young men like Jimmy. When Jimmy seduces Patsy's girlfriend, it is as though Jimmy, too, is engaging in macho one-upmanship and taking away his father's girlfriend. Then, when Jimmy pistol-whips Patsy, grips the man's balls and shoots out his eyes, the son is not only *killing for his father* (avenging the father's death and becoming a gangster like him), but also *killing his father*, castrating the old man who made him feel like a weak little boy.

The Beat That My Heart Skipped (De battre mon cœur s'est arrêté) (2005)

Directed by: Jacques Audiard
Written by: Jacques Audiard and Tonino Benacquista, from the screenplay *Fingers* by James Toback
Produced by: Pascal Caucheteux
Edited by: Juliette Welfling
Cinematography: Stéphane Fontaine
Cast: Romain Duris (*Thomas Seyr*), Niels Arestrup (*Robert Seyr*), Jonathan Zaccaï (*Fabrice*), Gilles Cohen (*Sami*), Linh Dan Pahm (*Miao Lin*)

Plot

Tom and his buddies Fabrice and Sami evict squatters from run-down Parisian apartments by releasing rats in the stairwells and using baseball bats on occupants' heads. The vacant buildings are then resold at a profit. Fabrice regularly cheats on his wife Aline and lies to her, claiming to be out with Tom, but when she gets wise to the deception, Tom and Aline begin having an affair behind Fabrice's back. Tom says he loves her, but she goes back to Fabrice. Tom's mother is deceased, but he aspires to become a concert pianist like her and hires a Vietnamese girl, piano prodigy Miao-Lin, to coach him on his playing. Wherever he goes, Tom listens to music on headphones and moves his fingers as if practising, causing his buddies to berate him for having his mind on music rather than on the business of evictions. Despite Tom's protests ('It's not about making money; it's about art'), Fabrice and Sami compel him to take part in a violent eviction on the night before his big audition, which he then fails. Furthermore, Tom discovers that his father has been murdered by a gangster named Minskov, and, two years later, after spotting Minskov on the street, Tom follows the man into a restroom where, in a vicious fight, he hits him with a briefcase, grabs his balls and puts a gun in his mouth. But Tom doesn't shoot. Instead, still bloody and bruised from the fight, Tom goes to the concert hall to hear a piano performance by Miao-Lin. Tom has become her manager and lover. Listening to her play, he closes his eyes and smiles, moving his fingers as if he himself is playing. He then opens his eyes, and she and he exchange loving glances.

Comments

On one of their nights terrorising squatters, Tom's friend Sami is himself bitten by a rat he loosed on others, much as Tom injures his own hand when he beats up one of his father's debtors. Metaphorically, if Tom continues along this same (self-) destructive path, he threatens to evict himself from home and from any future in the performing arts apart from the 'art' of violence. Tom remains in touch with his mother's artistic spirit by listening to tapes of her practice sessions, by running his fingers over the notes she played, and by playing the piano himself in his apartment. In this way, Tom's home becomes a kind of maternal womb of cultural nourishment. Even though Aline leaves Tom to go back to her philandering husband (just as Carol left Jimmy in *Fingers* to return to the unworthy Dreems), Tom is then lucky enough to meet Miao-Lin (a character with no equivalent in *Fingers*), who knows no French but speaks the same language of touch and music. As she coaches him on how to play the piano with discipline and passion, communicating physically to him how he should move his arms and hands, Tom reconnects with his concert-pianist mother and with his better self. (Interestingly, the actor in the role of Tom, Romain Duris, has an older sister who is a concert pianist. She taught him how to play for 30-second bursts while the camera is on his hands.) Because of Miao-Lin's love and inspiration, Tom does not condemn himself to a life of violence by taking vengeance in the end. Instead, he returns to his true home, a world of peace he once found only in his own apartment but which is now enlarged to fill the concert hall and wherever else music prevails.

Basic Instinct (1992)

Directed by: Paul Verhoeven
Written by: Joe Eszterhas
Produced by: Alan Marshall
Edited by: Frank J Urioste
Cinematography: Jan de Bont
Cast: Michael Douglas (*Nick Curran*), Sharon Stone (*Catherine Tramell*), George Dzundza (*Gus Moran*), Jeanne Tripplehorne (*Dr Beth Garner*)

Plot

A woman rides a man in bed, ties his hands to the bedpost, and at the moment of climax stabs him to death with an ice pick. Detective Nick Curran at first suspects Catherine Tramell, who was known to have been sleeping with the victim and who wrote a novel in which a man was killed in the exact same way. Nick himself begins a sexual relationship with Catherine. He claims that this is his way of investigating her, but she may have seduced and be manipulating *him*. Then, when Catherine's lesbian lover Roxy tries to run Nick down with a car (and afterwards dies in a crash), the police have reason to believe that Roxy was the murderer, having been driven to it by jealousy. However, when another ice-pick murder is committed, suspicion falls on Dr Beth Garner, Nick's police psychiatrist and lover. It turns out that Beth had had an obsessive affair with Catherine in the past, and now, after Beth's death, all the evidence points towards her as the jealous murderer of the men in Catherine's life. And yet, as Nick and Catherine make love at the end of the film, the camera moves down to reveal an ice pick under her bed....

Comments

In some classic film noirs, the femme fatale is counterbalanced by the 'good girl' who helps the detective-hero and comforts him in a wifely way. But in this neo-noir, even the good girl could be bad. Beth, the psychiatrist who aids Nick in solving the case (she 'profiles' the killer) and who helps him with his emotional problems, becomes a suspect in the killings and a potential femme fatale herself. *Basic Instinct* can be read as a film about rampant male paranoia, in which every female is feared as a threat to masculinity. Did Catherine do it, or Roxy, or Beth? It is as if, just by being a member of the opposite sex, these women fall under suspicion. When Nick says at one point, 'I'm not sure anymore that she did it,' his partner Gus replies, 'Which one are we talking about now?' Moreover, both Roxy and Beth seem to have slept with Catherine, a discovery which deeply disturbs Nick. Here lesbianism is feared as a sign of conspiracy, as if women interacting without a man must mean that they are plotting against him. The film's opening sex/murder scene, in which the woman is on top, ties up the man and impales him with an ice pick at her climax, exposes the male fear of a sexually active woman. It would kill him for her to be the dominant one, for him to feel passive, for her to take pleasure. If she were to become 'the man', he would feel unmanned. (We later see the flaccid penis on the dead male victim.)

As the detective-hero, Nick's goal is to solve the mystery of the enigmatic woman (is Catherine the killer?) but also to reassert male dominance over her in bed. 'I'll nail you,' he tells her, proclaiming both investigative and sexual mastery. One reason these women are a mystery is that they do not behave according to the 'good girl' role that men expect them to fit. In a sense, they are all 'phallic women' who seem to have grabbed the signs of masculine power and authority for themselves. Catherine smokes a cigarette when doing so is forbidden. Beth, Nick suspects, may have a gun in her pocket. Roxy, a butch lesbian, used a razor to kill her brothers and tries to run Nick down with a car. Any one of these phallic women could be the wielder of the ice pick. When Nick has sex with Catherine in the middle of the film, he positions himself above her, holds her arms above her head and attains his climax after assertive thrusting. Later, however, she rolls on top of him, ties up his hands and rides him while appearing to reach back for – an ice pick? No, but this is what the power of her sexuality has made him fear. At the end of the film, the ice pick revealed under her bed indicates that, despite their having exchanged positions of dominance during sex to their mutual satisfaction, he is still afraid.

Factoid

In his contract, Michael Douglas (Nick) stipulated that his sex organ must never be exposed to view. Sharon Stone (Catherine) did not have the same clause in her contract, as viewers of her infamous leg-uncrossing scene know.[85]

Basic Instinct 2 (2006)

Directed by: Michael Caton-Jones
Written by: Leora Barish and Henry Bean, based on characters created by Joe Eszterhas
Produced by: Mario F Kassar, Andrew G Vajna and Joel B Michaels
Edited by: John Scott and István Király
Cinematography: Gyula Pados
Cast: Sharon Stone (*Catherine Tramell*), David Morrissey (*Michael Glass*), Charlotte Rampling (*Milena Gardosh*), David Thewlis (*Roy Washburn*)

Plot

Catherine Tramell drives a sports car at 110 mph through London with a man's hand between her legs. At the moment of climax, the car shoots off a bridge and into the Thames River, where her male passenger drowns but she escapes. Psychoanalyst Michael Glass begins treating Catherine but seems inexorably drawn into her seduction and manipulation of him. All the people in Michael's life start showing up dead. His ex-wife's lover (Adam) is strangled in bed with a belt. The ex-wife herself (Denise) is found with her throat slashed. After Michael falls for Catherine and they have sex, her previous lover is found strangled. Finally, Michael decides that Catherine must be the murderer, but even as he holds her at gunpoint, she convinces him that a detective (Roy Washburn) did the killings. After Michael shoots Roy, Michael is arrested and put in an insane asylum, where Catherine visits him to present yet another theory: without his realising it at the time, Michael himself committed all the crimes.

Comments

Here is how Catherine describes the relationship between Michael and herself: 'Is the beautiful blonde... a serial killer?... Her analyst isn't sure, but he goes crazy trying to find out.' In this neo-noir, the detective-hero gets locked up for murder; the therapist goes mad. Rather than remaining objective, Michael begins to project his own desires onto Catherine, as when he leers at her bare legs during a therapy session. Catherine knows that he is looking and getting excited. Director Michael Caton-Jones describes her 'seduction' of Michael as kind of 'snake charming', a 'toying with his masculinity'.[86] Indeed, Catherine actually fondles a miniature model of the very building in which Michael has his office – a famously phallic building known as the 'Erotic Gherkin'. While Michael may think of himself as a high-powered analyst in his high-rise office, he is really losing control of his mind and giving way to his unconscious lusts and aggressions. 'Who's the patient and who's the doctor?' asks Catherine at one point, and she warns Michael, 'Maybe I'm acting out your unconscious impulses' – that is, if he is not unknowingly acting them out himself. Isn't it strange that Michael's ex-wife has her throat slashed after she revealed incriminating information about him to a reporter? How odd that this reporter, who was sleeping with Michael's ex-wife and about to publish his story, is silenced by means of strangulation. And there is peculiar timing in the fact that Catherine's former lover ends up dead right after Michael sees them in bed together and then begins sleeping with her himself. As Michael and Catherine are having sex, she slips a leather belt around his neck and he climaxes as a result of the erotic asphyxiation. Earlier, Michael had diagnosed Catherine's mental illness as 'risk addiction':

'The greater the risk, the greater the proof of her omnipotence... I suspect the only limit for her would be her own death.' But it is Michael himself who seems drawn to thrill-seeking sex taken to the very brink of death. He doesn't want to cure Catherine of her murderous desires and suicidal urges. Instead, he wants to join her in sex as an extreme sport.

Factoid

According to director Michael Caton-Jones, the identity of the killer remains 'ambiguous' in the end, a kind of Rorschach blot: 'It's up to you, the audience. [The killer] can be whoever you want it to be. And it will tell you more about yourself than about the film.'[87]

Open Your Eyes (Abre los ojos) (1997)

Directed by: Alejandro Amenábar
Written by: Alejandro Amenábar and Mateo Gil
Produced by: Fernando Bovaira and José Luis Cuerda
Edited by: María Elena Sáinz de Rozas
Cinematography: Hans Burman
Cast: Eduardo Noriega (*César*), Penélope Cruz (*Sofía*), Chete Lera (*Antonio*), Fele Martínez (*Pelayo*), Najwa Nimri (*Nuria*), Gérard Barray (*Duvernois*)

Vanilla Sky (2001)

Directed by: Cameron Crowe
Written by: Cameron Crowe, based on the film *Abre los ojos* written by Alejandro Amenábar and Mateo Gil
Produced by: Tom Cruise, Paula Wagner and Cameron Crowe
Edited by: Joe Hutshing
Cinematography: John Toll
Cast: Tom Cruise (*David Aames*), Penélope Cruz (*Sofía Serrano*), Cameron Diaz (*Julie Gianni*), Kurt Russell (*McCabe*), Jason Lee (*Brian Shelby*), Noah Taylor (*Edmund Ventura*)

Plot

César (David in the 2001 version) is a wealthy and narcissistic young man. At his birthday party, he gives his latest girlfriend Nuria/Julie the brush-off and steals another woman, Sofía, away from his best friend Pelayo/Brian. Back at her apartment, César falls romantically in love with Sofía, but the next morning he allows Nuria to pick him up in her car, which the jealous ex-girlfriend then deliberately crashes, killing herself and horribly disfiguring César. The doctors do their best but are unable to repair his monstrous facial scars, and the blank-faced prosthetic mask they offer him as an alternative seems in its own way to be equally frightening. When César goes to see Sofía again at a nightclub, she now seems more attracted to Pelayo than to him, and when the three friends go their separate ways later that night, César imagines Pelayo meeting up with Sofía afterwards to take her in his arms. A drunken and despairing César passes out in front of Sofía's apartment. When he next opens his eyes, everything is different: not only is Sofía in love with him again, but the surgeons are suddenly able to restore his face to its original manly perfection. However, when he gets up from bed one night to look at himself in the bathroom mirror, César sees the same scars fracturing his face. Luckily, he then wakes up again to find himself with a normal face, but upon returning to bed discovers that his beloved Sofía has been replaced by the femme fatale Nuria, whom he smothers with a pillow. César goes looking for Sofía, but everyone tells him Nuria is Sofía, and Nuria's face has replaced Sofía's in all the photos and drawings he has of her. César is arrested for having murdered 'Sofía'. As he tells his life story to prison psychiatrist Antonio/McCabe, César seems to figure out what really happened. After the disfiguring accident, César had his body cryogenically preserved by a company called Life Extension. This company has allowed him to live a virtual reality in his head, a wish-fulfilment fantasy that was spliced into his real life from the moment he passed out in front of Sofía's apartment. The recurring facial scars and the re-appearances of Nuria were just glitches in the program, elements from his unconscious that can now be thoroughly repressed so that he can live the perfect fantasy life, as César is told by company doctor Duvernois/Ventura. However, César chooses to kiss his dream Sofía goodbye and to jump off the roof of the company building.

Comments

Abre los ojos begins with the sound of a woman's voice (speaking as a recorded message on César's alarm clock) telling him to 'open your eyes', and the film seems designed to bring him to a realisation of who he really is. Yes, meeting the wonderful Sofía at his birthday party makes César think that he can be reborn as a better person through his romance with her, but he has just dumped yet another girlfriend (Nuria) and he can't resist having sex with her again, which is why he lets her pick him up in her car. The facial scars he gets from the terrible car accident are just the external signs of the moral monster César really is inside. Whether it is owing to God or just guilt, his conscience won't let César begin a romance with Sofía until he pays for what he has done to Nuria and the other women he has exploited in his past. Furthermore, César has always prided himself on having the looks and the girls that his best friend Pelayo cannot attain, so it is poetic justice when César's face is disfigured and he loses Sofía to the friend from whom he had originally stolen her.

When César begins courting Sofía again, he cannot trust her because he lacks trust in himself. His uncertainty over how she will respond to his scarred face is conveyed in the park scene where he sees her face covered in white mime make-up: what does she really think of him behind her blank mask? And César himself wears a blank facial prosthetic to his nightclub rendezvous with her, for he doesn't know whether he's a man or a monster behind his mask. Later, while making love to Sofía, César's doubts about her get the better of him, which is why he sees her 'change' into the femme fatale Nuria. (It is possible that actually having sex with the girl of his dreams reminds César of all his past one-night-stands; that he cannot reconcile romance with physical intercourse.) While still thrusting into Nuria, César smothers her by putting a pillow over her face (blanking out the untrustworthy woman he doesn't want to see), and as a physical manifestation of this immoral act, he then sees monstrous fractures open up in his own face. However, when the Life Extension company tells him that he can smooth out all the glitches in his virtual reality and live the perfect fantasy life, César refuses, for he has finally learned *not* to repress the interruptions from his unconscious. These have taught him that, in order to be his truest self, he must respond to the reality of others and feel their pushback against his narcissistic fantasy. Thus, when he kisses his dream Sofía goodbye, it is because he treasures the memory of the real Sofía and will no longer settle for anything less. Jumping off the company roof, César shows that he is ready to register the ultimate pushback against the self – death. His reward comes when a real woman (not just his fantasy) tells him to 'open your eyes', awakening him to a life in the future – or to the afterlife.

Director Cameron Crowe, who began his career as a rock journalist, has described *Vanilla Sky* as a 'cover version' of *Abre los ojos*, as if Amenábar's original film were a popular song that is now going to be performed by a different band. In fact, this description is also apt in the sense that Crowe's film is very much *about* the effect of popular culture on our lives: David's 'life… is defined like so many of us… by pop culture. But where does a real life begin, and where does pop culture end?'[88] Pop culture can be a threat if its alluring images become addictive substitutes for reality, as when David mistakes sex in his playboy pad with model-pretty Julie for a genuine relationship: 'What is love in a world that's just fuelled by pop culture and a lot of visions of easy sexual conquest?'[89] David must learn to resist the seduction of femme fatales like Julie (with her alluring blue eyes that match the blue of her fancy car) and the seductive wiles of a company like Life Extension, which sells him a vision of a perfect life that is in fact only a virtual reality, empty and soulless. In making its pitch, the company uses one of David's favourite pop songs, the Beach Boys' 'Good Vibrations', to *move* him to buy, but David grows to realise that the fantasy life they have sold him *does not live up* to the feeling in the song. Here is a case of pop culture that once inspired and now keeps alive the dream of a better life. It is a song that helps to *save* David from settling for a lesser virtual reality and to feed his desire for something real: 'It's an emotional song that's been... corrupted by being used in commercials... and it's been played a lot, but wouldn't it be great if this great song can get kind of buffed and polished and viewed in a completely different context?'[90] Thus pop songs and media images are not always cheap fantasies separating us from true reality. They may instead lead us towards a higher reality, as when David sees the photos of Sofia in her apartment and 'falls in love with the image of a girl living a real life, a life more real than his life'.[91] At the beginning of the film, David is dreaming in bed while Audrey Hepburn in the film *Sabrina* plays in the background on his TV. This filmic image of what love can be inspires him to fall in love with the actual Sofia, to see her as the girl of his dreams. And when he loses Sofia, he recreates her in his mind as part of the Life Extension fantasy, using *Sabrina* to help him imagine her. In the end, though, he realises that the image is not enough. As he is falling from the roof he has jumped off, the images of his life – especially ones of Sofia – flash through his mind. They are mere images he must leave behind, but they are also ideal images pointing him to a higher reality in the next life.

Factoid

Rather than use digital trickery to fake an impression of deserted streets in the scene where Tom Cruise runs through an empty Times Square, the filmmakers actually cleared all the people and traffic from this New York City location, which is normally one of the busiest and most crowded places in the world.

Infernal Affairs (Mou gaan dou) (2002)

Directed by: Andrew Lau and Alan Mak
Written by: Alan Mak and Felix Chong
Produced by: Andrew Lau
Edited by: Danny Pang and Pang Ching Hei
Cinematography: Andrew Lau and Lai Yiu Fai
Cast: Andy Lau (*Inspector Lau Kin Ming*), Tony Leung (*Chan Wing Yan*), Anthony Wong (*SP Wong Chi Shing*), Eric Tsang (*Hon Sam*), Kelly Chen (*Dr Lee Sum Yee*), Sammi Cheng (*Mary*)

The Departed (2006)

Directed by: Martin Scorsese
Written by: William Monahan, based on the screenplay *Infernal Affairs* by Alan Mak and Felix Chong
Produced by: Brad Pitt, Brad Grey and Graham King
Edited by: Thelma Schoonmaker
Cinematography: Michael Ballhaus
Cast: Leonard DiCaprio (*Billy Costigan*), Matt Damon (*Colin*), Jack Nicholson (*Costello*), Mark Wahlberg (*Dignam*), Martin Sheen (*Queenan*), Vera Farmiga (*Madolyn*)

Plot

A mob boss (Sam in the original version/Costello in the remake) places gang member Lau/Colin as a mole inside the police force. Police chief Wong/Queenan gets undercover cop Chan/Billy to infiltrate the gang. Because of his inside information, Billy is able to tip off the cops about one of the gang's illegal deals, but thanks to Colin's advance warning, the gang gets rid of the evidence before they are caught and so cannot be arrested. In an effort to discover the other mole, Colin has police captain Queenan tailed to a rooftop meeting with Billy and then calls in the gang to deal with them. Billy escapes without being seen, but Queenan is tortured to reveal Billy's identity (he doesn't) and then thrown from the roof, landing in a bloody heap at Billy's feet on the street below. Colin (the mob mole) wants to protect his identity as a cop and so he lures his gang boss Costello to a meeting and kills him. Colin discovers that Billy is the police informant, but Billy figures out that Colin is the mob mole. In order to protect himself, Colin wipes the computer file that proves Billy is an undercover cop, but in a climactic rooftop scene, Billy holds Colin at gunpoint, determined to arrest him and prove who each man really is. Another cop intervenes, shooting Billy dead, but when this 'cop' reveals himself to be a mob mole like Colin, Colin kills the man. At the end of *Infernal Affairs* (international release version), Lau technically gets away with murder, but he has created a living hell for himself: the rest of his life will be tormented by a fear of exposure and by the knowledge that the image of himself as a good cop is a hollow sham. At the end of *The Departed*, Colin doesn't get to masquerade as a heroic policeman for long: he is killed by another cop in retaliation for his role in the killing of Captain Queenan.

Comments

Film noirs in which police go undercover as criminals often blur the line between cops and crooks. The neo-noir *Infernal Affairs* pushes this tendency to an extreme, making that differentiating line all but invisible. Not only does a cop (Chan) infiltrate a triad gang, but a gang member (Lau) successfully passes as a cop; and, what's more, each mole is assigned by his boss to find the mole in the other organisation. Since they were both placed in deep cover 11 years ago when they were young men, Chan and Lau have been living a life of duplicity for so long that they are losing track of who they really are. To prove his street cred as a gangster, Chan has had to commit acts of violence unbecoming of a police officer, and he is being treated by a psychiatrist for antisocial aggression and schizoid tendencies: 'Do you think I'm a good guy or a bad guy?' Chan's fingers are constantly jittering, and it's not always clear whether this is the secret tapping of Morse code or just a symptom of mental breakdown. When his own boss, police superintendent Wong, gives him a watch as a birthday present, the paranoid Chan first assumes it is a listening device and 'jokes' that they should stick a wire into his body so that he can become a living 'bug', the perfect snitch. Later, when head mobster Sam suspects that Chan may be hiding a bug, Sam breaks the plaster cast on Chan's already broken arm, inflicting further damage on a man who is in fact a kind of walking wire. Constantly surveilling others while afraid he is being watched, rootlessly moving from place to place and changing identities depending on who is on the other end of his cell-phone calls, Chan is losing himself to a technology of suspicion, evasion and deception. When the computer record of his true identity as an undercover cop is deleted by Lau, it is almost as though Chan's very self has been erased.

As for Lau, the gangster pretending to be a cop, he is suffering from a similar identity crisis in which 'he starts to forget which one is the real him', as his fiancée Mary says. Unlike Chan, the outwardly respectable Lau has a beloved and a home to help root him in goodness, and he wants to obliterate his own criminal past to become a thoroughly legitimate cop. To stabilise his identity as a good guy, Lau lures his own mobster boss Sam into a trap and shoots him dead. Ironically, this act of unpoliceman-like violence, this cold-blooded killing, is applauded by his fellow officers and gets Lau promoted. If this is what it means to be a cop, what difference is there between it and being a gangster? In the film's climactic scene between Lau and Chan on a rooftop, Lau sees a blurry reflection in a glass skyscraper: the image could be himself or Chan, the criminal-as-cop or the cop-as-criminal. When another gangster mole in the police department shoots Chan, Lau shoots the mole. He is killing the 'mole' side of himself so that he can be a good cop, but he is also killing to cover up the truth about his connection to the gang. In the film's sequel (*Infernal Affairs III*), Lau will go on to murder another suspected mole in order to protect his own image as a good cop – an image proven false by that very murder.

In *The Departed*, director Martin Scorsese remakes the tale by emphasising the powerful influence of fathers on sons. Gang boss Costello first 'adopts' Colin when he is just a boy. When Colin sees Costello extort protection money from a grocer and lay sexual claim to the man's daughter, the example is set: 'No one gives it to you. You have to take it.' Virility is proven by dominating others, as in the football game between police and firemen in which a triumphant Colin (now undercover as a cop) calls the losers 'homos'. To rise in the organisation (whether this be the mob or the police), you must castrate the competition, as shown in the scene where Costello has a man's severed hand in a plastic bag. 'A lot of people had to die for me to be me,' Costello admits, and Colin mirrors his gangster father-figure's ruthless ambition by killing those who threaten to take away the spoils of his victory. If anyone were to expose him as a mob mole, Colin would lose the luxury condo and the wealthy woman (Madolyn) he has gained from being a respected and highly promoted detective on the police force. But viewing the world as one of male rivalry and cutthroat competition tends to induce fears of weakness and rampant paranoia. Colin sometimes finds himself impotent with Madolyn and, at other times, a cell-phone call from Costello interrupts his lovemaking as the gang boss threatens to expose him and take away everything he has if Colin will not do his bidding. At a meeting in a porn theatre, Costello exhibits a giant fake penis to Colin, threatening him with his greater virility. When the father's lesson to the son is that this is a dog-eat-dog world, the two inevitably become rivals over who will be top dog. When Colin finds out that Costello has informed on other members of his own gang to the FBI, the father tries to reassure the son ('You know I'd never give *you* up'), but mutual distrust leads to a shootout in which the son kills the father. In the end, Colin's girlfriend Madolyn finds out that he has been a member of Costello's gang and, even though she is pregnant with Colin's son, she walks right by him and out of his life forever. She does not want their son to be influenced by a father like Colin.

Factoid

To elicit reactions of genuine surprise from his co-stars, Jack Nicholson spilled lighter fluid and set a table on fire without forewarning Leonardo DiCaprio; he also pulled out the huge fake phallus in front of Matt Damon in the porn theatre without telling him in advance.

RECOMMENDED FILMS FOR FURTHER VIEWING

Breathless (1959)
Shoot the Piano Player (1960)
Cape Fear (1962)
The Killers (1964)
Alphaville (1965)
Mickey One (1965)
Blow Up (1966)
Harper (1966)
Mister Buddwing (1966)
Bonnie and Clyde (1967)
The Butcher (1970)
The Conformist (1970)
The Honeymoon Killers (1970)
Performance (1970)
The Spider's Stratagem (1970)
Dirty Harry (1971)
Klute (1971)
The Offence (1972)
Prime Cut (1972)
Badlands (1973)
The Long Goodbye (1973)
The Conversation (1974)

The Parallax View (1974)
Thieves Like Us (1974)
Farewell, My Lovely (1975)
Night Moves (1975)
The Passenger (1975)
The Killer Inside Me (1976)
Mr. Klein (1976)
Obsession (1976)
Taxi Driver (1976)
The American Friend (1977)
The Driver (1978)
Eyes of Laura Mars (1978)
Winter Kills (1979)
Bad Timing: A Sensual Obsession (1980)
The Long Good Friday (1980)
Blow Out (1981)
Cutter's Way (1981)
Eyewitness (1981)
Ms .45 (1981)
Thief (1981)
True Confessions (1981)
Dead Men Don't Wear Plaid (1982)
Scarface (1983)
Against All Odds (1984)
Body Double (1984)
Choose Me (1984)
Hit Man (1984)
Once Upon a Time in America (1984)
Tightrope (1984)
After Hours (1985)
Year of the Dragon (1985)
At Close Range (1986)
Angel Heart (1987)

Recommended Films for Further Viewing

The Big Easy (1987)
Black Widow (1987)
Fatal Attraction (1987)
No Way Out (1987)
Apartment Zero (1988)
Jack's Back (1988)
Stormy Monday (1988)
Batman (1989)
Black Rain (1989)
Dead Calm (1989)
Sea of Love (1989)
Bad Influence (1990)
La Femme Nikita (1990)
The Grifters (1990)
Impulse (1990)
Jacob's Ladder (1990)
The Krays (1990)
Miller's Crossing (1990)
Pacific Heights (1990)
State of Grace (1990)
The Adjuster (1991)
Barton Fink (1991)
Cape Fear (1991)
Dead Again (1991)
Naked Lunch (1991)
Point Break (1991)
A Rage in Harlem (1991)
Bad Lieutenant (1992)
Deep Cover (1992)
Final Analysis (1992)
Guncrazy (1992)
Love Crimes (1992)
One False Move (1992)

Single White Female (1992)
Swoon (1992)
Twin Peaks: Fire Walk with Me (1992)
Carlito's Way (1993)
Fatal Instinct (1993)
Malice (1993)
Point of No Return (1993)
Red Rock West (1993)
Rising Sun (1993)
Romeo Is Bleeding (1993)
Sonatine (1993)
True Romance (1993)
The Crow (1994)
Exotica (1994)
The Last Seduction (1994)
Natural Born Killers (1994)
Frisk (1995)
Get Shorty (1995)
Ghost in the Shell (1995)
Heat (1995)
Lord of Illusions (1995)
Shallow Grave (1995)
Strange Days (1995)
Twelve Monkeys (1995)
Last Man Standing (1996)
Lone Star (1996)
Mission: Impossible (1996)
Mulholland Falls (1996)
Thesis (1996)
Face (1997)
The Game (1997)
Gattaca (1997)
Insomnia (1997)

Recommended Films for Further Viewing

Jackie Brown (1997)
The Spanish Prisoner (1997)
U Turn (1997)
The Big Lebowski (1998)
Clay Pigeons (1998)
Dark City (1998)
Lock, Stock and Two Smoking Barrels (1998)
Pi (1998)
Place Vendôme (1998)
Run Lola Run (1998)
A Simple Plan (1998)
Snake Eyes (1998)
Wild Things (1998)
8mm (1999)
Arlington Road (1999)
eXistenZ (1999)
Eyes Wide Shut (1999)
Fight Club (1999)
L'Humanité (1999)
American Psycho (2000)
The Cell (2000)
Crimson Rivers (2000)
Sexy Beast (2000)
Snatch (2000)
Suzhou River (2000)
The Way of the Gun (2000)
The Deep End (2001)
Donnie Darko (2001)
From Hell (2001)
The Pledge (2001)
Training Day (2001)
City of God (2002)
Insomnia (2002)

Irreversible (2002)
Minority Report (2002)
Road to Perdition (2002)
The Salton Sea (2002)
The Cooler (2003)
In the Cut (2003)
The Machinist (2004)
Mysterious Skin (2004)
Primer (2004)
Suspect Zero (2004)
The Aura (2005)
Brick (2005)
A History of Violence (2005)
The Jacket (2005)
Kiss Kiss Bang Bang (2005)
The Three Burials of Melquiades Estrada (2005)
Where the Truth Lies (2005)
Casino Royale (2006)
Déjà Vu (2006)
The Good German (2006)
Hollywoodland (2006)
Lucky Number Slevin (2006)
Renaissance (2006)
A Scanner Darkly (2006)
Southland Tales (2006)
V for Vendetta (2006)
Eastern Promises (2007)
The Lookout (2007)
Perfect Stranger (2007)
Crank: High Voltage (2009)
Public Enemies (2009)
Shutter Island (2010)

BIBLIOGRAPHY

Ballinger, Alex and Danny Graydon, *The Rough Guide to Film Noir*, London: Rough Guides, 2007.
Bould, Mark, *Film Noir: From Berlin to Sin City*, London: Wallflower Press, 2005.
Brode, Douglas, *Money, Women, and Guns: Crime Movies from Bonnie and Clyde to the Present*, New York: Citadel Press, 1995.
Buckland, Warren (ed), *Puzzle Films: Complex Storytelling in Contemporary Cinema*, Chichester, UK: Wiley-Blackwell, 2009.
Butler, David, *Jazz Noir: Listening to Music from Phantom Lady to The Last Seduction*, Westport, CT: Praeger, 2002.
Cameron, Ian (ed), *The Book of Film Noir*, New York: Continuum, 1993.
Chibnall, Steve and Robert Murphy (eds), *British Crime Cinema*, London: Routledge, 1999.
Conard, Mark T (ed), *The Philosophy of Neo-Noir*, Lexington: University Press of Kentucky, 2007.
Derry, Charles, *The Suspense Thriller: Films in the Shadow of Alfred Hitchcock*, Jefferson, NC: McFarland, 1988.
Dixon, Wheeler Winston, *Film Noir and the Cinema of Paranoia*, New Brunswick, NJ: Rutgers UP, 2009.
Duncan, Paul, *Film Noir: Films of Trust and Betrayal*, 2nd ed, Harpenden, UK: Pocket Essentials, 2006.
Fulwood, Neil, *One Hundred Violent Films That Changed Cinema*, London: BT Batsford, 2003.
Gates, Philippa, *Detecting Men: Masculinity and the Hollywood Detective Film*, Albany: State University of New York Press, 2006.
Gifford, Barry, *Out of the Past: Adventures in Film Noir*, Jackson: University Press of Mississippi, 2001.

Grant, John, *Noir Movies: Facts, Figures & Fun*, London: AAPPL Artists' and Photographers' Press, 2006.

Hanson, Helen, *Hollywood Heroines: Women in Film Noir and the Female Gothic Film*, London: IB Tauris, 2007.

Hardy, Phil (ed), *The Gangster Film*, Woodstock, NY: Overlook Press, 1998.

Hillier, Jim and Alastair Phillips, *100 Film Noirs*, Basingstoke, UK: Palgrave Macmillan, 2009.

Hirsh, Foster, *Detours and Lost Highways: A Map of Neo-Noir*, New York: Limelight Editions, 1999.

Holm, DK, *Film Soleil*, Harpenden, UK: Pocket Essentials, 2005.

Hughes, Howard, *Crime Wave: The Filmgoers' Guide to the Great Crime Movies*, London: IB Taurus, 2006.

Hughes, Lloyd, *The Rough Guide to Gangster Movies*, London: Rough Guides, 2005.

Kaplan, E Ann (ed), *Women in Film Noir*, new ed, London: British Film Institute, 1998.

Leitch, Thomas, *Crime Films*, Cambridge: Cambridge University Press, 2002.

Mainon, Dominique and James Ursini, *Cinema of Obsession: Erotic Fixation and Love Gone Wrong in the Movies*, New York: Limelight Editions, 2007.

Martin, Nina, *Sexy Thrills: Undressing the Erotic Thriller*, Urbana: University of Illinois Press, 2007.

Martin, Richard, *Mean Streets and Raging Bulls: The Legacy of Film Noir in Contemporary American Cinema*, new ed, Lanham, MD: Scarecrow Press, 1999.

Mason, Fran, *American Gangster Cinema: From Little Caesar to Pulp Fiction*, New York: Palgrave Macmillan, 2002.

Maxfield, James F, *The Fatal Woman: Sources of Male Anxiety in American Film Noir, 1941–1991*, Madison, NJ: Farleigh Dickinson University Press, 1996.

Mayer, Geoff and Brian McDonnell, *Encyclopedia of Film Noir*, Westport, CT: Greenwood Press, 2007.

McCarty, John, *Bullets over Broadway: The American Gangster Picture from the Silents to The Sopranos*, Cambridge, MA: Da Capo Press, 2004.

Meehan, Paul, *Tech-Noir*, Jefferson, NC: McFarland, 2008.

Naremore, James, *More than Night: Film Noir in Its Contexts*, revised ed, Berkeley: University of California Press, 2008.

Oliver, Kelly and Benigno Trigo, *Noir Anxiety*, Minneapolis: University of Minnesota Press, 2003.

Pappas, Charles, *It's a Bitter Little World: The Smartest, Toughest, Nastiest Quotes from Film Noir*, Cincinnati, OH: Writer's Digest Books, 2005.

Rafter, Nicole, *Shots in the Mirror: Crime Films and Society*, 2nd ed, Oxford: Oxford University Press, 2006.

Rich, Nathaniel, *San Francisco Noir: The City in Film Noir from 1940 to the Present*, New York: Little Bookroom, 2005.

Robson, Eddie, *Film Noir*, London: Virgin Books, 2005.

Schwartz, Ronald, *Neo-Noir: The New Film Noir Style from Psycho to Collateral*, Lanham, MD: Scarecrow Press, 2005.

Schwartz, Ronald, *Noir, Now and Then: Film Noir Originals and Remakes (1944–1999)*, Westport, CT: Greenwood Press, 2001.

Silver, Alain and Elizabeth Ward (eds), *Film Noir: An Encyclopedic Reference to the American Style*, 3rd ed, Woodstock, NY: Overlook Press, 1992.

Silver, Alain and James Ursini, *L.A. Noir: The City as Character*, Santa Monica, CA: Santa Monica Press, 2005.

Smith, Jim, *Gangster Films*, London: Virgin Books, 2004.

Spicer, Andrew (ed), *European Film Noir*, Manchester: Manchester University Press, 2007.

Spicer, Andrew, *Film Noir*, Harlow, UK: Longman, 2002.

Thompson, Kirsten Moana, *Crime Films: Investigating the Scene*, London: Wallflower Press, 2007.

Wager, Jans B, *Dames in the Driver's Seat: Rereading Film Noir*, Austin: University of Texas Press, 2005.

Williams, Linda Ruth, *The Erotic Thriller in Contemporary Cinema*, Bloomington: Indiana University Press, 2005.

NOTES

1. Raymond Chandler, Introduction, *The Simple Art of Murder*, New York: Houghton Mifflin, 1950.
2. James Naremore, *More than Night: Film Noir in Its Contexts*, revised ed., Berkeley: University of California Press, 2008, p. 282.
3. Wheeler Winston Dixon, *Film Noir and the Cinema of Paranoia*, New Brunswick, NJ: Rutgers University Press, 2009, p. 1.
4. Jim Hillier and Alastair Phillips, *100 Film Noirs*, Basingstoke, UK: Palgrave Macmillan, 2009, pp. 5, 8.
5. Mark Bould, *Film Noir: From Berlin to Sin City*, London: Wallflower Press, 2005, p. 115.
6. William Friedkin, Director's Audiocommentary, *The French Connection* DVD, Twentieth Century Fox Home Entertainment, 2005.
7. Martin Scorsese in Ian Christie, 'Scorsese: Faith under Pressure', *Sight and Sound*, vol. 16, no. 11 (November 2006), p. 14.
8. Paul Schrader in Foster Hirsch, *Detours and Lost Highways: A Map of Neo-Noir*, New York: Limelight Editions, 1999, p. 2.
9. Robert Towne in Michael Eaton, *Chinatown*, London: British Film Institute, 1997, p. 67.
10. Ibid., p. 65.
11. Martin Scorsese, Director's Audiocommentary, *Taxi Driver* LD, Criterion, 1991.
12. Paul Schrader, *Collected Screenplays 1*, London: Faber and Faber, 2002, p. 48.
13. Paul Schrader in Kevin Jackson (ed.), *Schrader on Schrader*, London: Faber and Faber, 1990, p. 119.
14. Ridley Scott in James Clarke, *Ridley Scott*, London: Virgin Books, 2002, p. 83.

15 Stephen Rea in Carole Zucker, *In the Company of Actors: Reflections on the Craft of Acting*, London: A&C Black, 1999, p. 115.
16 Christopher McQuarrie, *The Usual Suspects*, London: Faber and Faber, 2000, p. xi.
17 Brian McDonnell in Geoff Mayer and Brian McDonnell, *Encyclopedia of Film Noir*, Westport, CT: Greenwood Press, 2007, p. 381.
18 Frank Miller in Frank Miller and Robert Rodriguez, *Frank Miller's Sin City: The Making of the Movie*, Austin, TX: Troublemaker Publisher, 2005, p. 16.
19 Ibid., p. 16.
20 Zack Snyder in Peter Aperlo, *Watchmen: The Film Companion*, London: Titan Books, 2009, p. 68.
21 Jackie Earle Haley in ibid., p. 67.
22 Dashiell Hammett, *Complete Novels*, New York: Library of America, 1999, p. 135.
23 Joel Coen in William G Luhr (ed.), *The Coen Brothers' Fargo*, Cambridge: Cambridge University Press, 2004, p. 122.
24 Laura Miller, 'The Banality of Virtue', *Salon.com*, no. 9 (9–22 March 1996).
25 Frances McDormand in Josh Levine, *The Coen Brothers: The Story of Two American Filmmakers*, Toronto: ECW Press, 2000, p. 127.
26 Joel Coen in William Rodney Allen (ed.), *The Coen Brothers: Interviews*, Jackson: University Press of Mississippi, 2006, p. 153.
27 Brian De Palma in Gavin Smith, 'Dream Project: The Name of the Game is Déjà Vu in *Femme Fatale*', vol. 38, no. 6 (November–December 2002), p. 28.
28 William Friedkin in Allan Hunter, *Gene Hackman*, New York: St. Martin's Press, 1987, p. 71.
29 William Friedkin, Director's Audiocommentary, *The French Connection* DVD, Twentieth Century Fox Home Entertainment, 2005.
30 Ibid.
31 William Friedkin, Director's Audiocommentary, *Cruising* DVD, Warner Home Video, 2007.
32 William Friedkin, Director's Audiocommentary, *To Live and Die in L.A.* DVD, MGM Home Entertainment, 2003.
33 Mike Hodges, Director's Audiocommentary, *Get Carter* DVD, Warner Home Video, 2000.
34 Paul Mayersberg, quoted in Steven Paul Davies, *Get Carter and Beyond: The Cinema of Mike Hodges*, London: BT Batsford, 2002, p. 165.

35 Mike Hodges, Audiocommentary, *I'll Sleep When I'm Dead* DVD, Momentum Pictures, 2005.
36 Trevor Preston, ibid.
37 Mike Hodges, ibid.
38 Laura Dern in Colin Odell and Michelle Le Blanc, *David Lynch*, Harpenden, UK: Kamera Books, 2007, p. 126.
39 Michael Mann, Director's Audiocommentary, *Collateral* DVD, DreamWorks Home Entertainment, 2004.
40 Michael Mann, Director's Audiocommentary, *Miami Vice* DVD, Universal Studios Home Entertainment, 2006.
41 Ibid.
42 Christopher Nolan, Audiocommentary, *Following* DVD, Columbia TriStar Home Entertainment, 2001.
43 Ibid.
44 Christopher Nolan in Daniel Argent, 'Remembering *Memento*', *Creative Screenwriting*, vol. 9, no. 1 (January–February 2002), p. 51.
45 Christopher Nolan in Geoff Boucher, 'Christopher Nolan on "Dark Knight"', Hero Complex Blog, *Los Angeles Times*, 27 October 2008.
46 Steven Soderbergh in Anthony Kaufman (ed.), *Steven Soderbergh: Interviews*, Jackson: University Press of Mississippi, 2002, p. 131.
47 Ibid., p. 82.
48 Ibid., p. 72.
49 Ibid., p. 132.
50 Lem Dobbs, Audiocommentary, *The Limey* DVD, Artisan Home Entertainment, 2000.
51 Quentin Tarantino in Gerald Peary (ed.), *Quentin Tarantino: Interviews*, Jackson: University Press of Mississippi, 1998, pp. 33, 45.
52 Salome Jens in Jerry Oppenheimer and Jack Vitek, *Idol: Rock Hudson: The True Story of an American Film Hero*, New York: Villard Books, 1986, p. 88.
53 Kathryn Bigelow in Pam Cook, 'Blue Steel', *Monthly Film Bulletin*, vol. 57 (November 1990), p. 312.
54 'Fiber bundles go where no camera has gone', *American Cinematographer*, vol. 70, no. 5 (1989), pp. 99–102.
55 Philip Brophy, *100 Modern Soundtracks*, London: British Film Institute, 2004, p. 48.

56 Carl Franklin, Director's Audiocommentary, *Devil in a Blue Dress* DVD, Sony Pictures, 2006.
57 Andy and Larry Wachowski, Directors' Audiocommentary, *Bound* DVD, Republic Pictures, 2000.
58 Jean-Pierre Melville, 'Melville on *Le Samouraï*', Brochure Insert, *Le Samouraï* DVD, Criterion Collection, 2005, pp. 21–2.
59 Ibid., p. 20.
60 Bertrand Tavernier in Stephen Hay, *Bertrand Tavernier: The Film-Maker of Lyon*, London: IB Tauris, 2000, p. 95.
61 Jack Stevenson, *Lars von Trier*, London: British Film Institute, 2002, p. 34.
62 Lars von Trier in Jan Lumholdt (ed.), *Lars von Trier: Interviews*, Jackson: University Press of Mississippi, 2003, p. 43.
63 Takeshi Kitano in Gavin Smith, 'Takeshi Talks', *Film Comment*, vol. 34, no. 2 (March–April 1998), p. 32.
64 Ibid., p. 32.
65 Alejandro González Iñárritu in Karen Durbin, 'Is Order Chronological or Emotional?' *New York Times*, 23 November 2003.
66 Olivier Assayas in David Thompson, 'Power Games, *Sight and Sound*, vol. 14, no. 5 (May 2004), p. 31.
67 Chan-wook Park in Liese Spencer, 'Revenger's Tragedy', *Sight and Sound*, vol. 14, no. 10 (October 2004), p. 20.
68 Chan-wook Park in Jonathan Romney, 'Sympathy for the Devil', *Artforum*, May 2006, p. 277.
69 Pedro Almodóvar in Frédéric Strauss (ed.), *Almodóvar on Almodóvar*, revised edition, London: Faber and Faber, 2006.
70 Julia Lovell in Eileen Chang, Wang Hui Ling, and James Schamus, *Lust, Caution: The Story, the Screenplay, and the Making of the Film*, New York: Pantheon Books, 2007, pp. 237, 234.
71 James Schamus in ibid., pp. xi–xii.
72 David Mamet in Dan Yakir, 'The Postman's Words', *Film Comment*, vol. 17, no. 2 (March–April 1981), p. 21.
73 Jessica Lange in Dan Yakir, 'Jessica Lange: From Kong to Cain', *Film Comment*, vol. 17, no. 2 (March–April 1981), p. 29.
74 Anthony Minghella in Timothy Bricknell (ed.), *Minghella on Minghella*, London: Faber and Faber, 2005, p. 38.
75 Anthony Minghella in Daniel Argent, 'The Talented Mister: An Interview

with Anthony Minghella', *Creative Screenwriting*, vol. 7, no. 1 (January–February 2000), p. 64.

76 Anthony Minghella, Director's Audiocommentary, *The Talented Mr. Ripley* DVD, Paramount Pictures, 2000.

77 John Frankenheimer in Gerald Pratley, *The Films of John Frankenheimer*, Bethlehem, PA: Lehigh University Press and London: Cygnus Arts, 1998, p. 40.

78 Jonathan Demme in David Thompson, 'Mind Control', *Sight and Sound*, vol. 14, no. 12 (December 2004), pp. 14, 18.

79 Ibid., p. 14.

80 John Boorman in Michel Ciment, *John Boorman*, trans. Gilbert Adair, London: Faber and Faber, 1986, p. 76.

81 Ibid., p.73.

82 John Boorman, *Adventures of a Suburban Boy*, London: Faber and Faber, 2003, pp. 135–6.

83 Brian Helgeland, Director's Audiocommentary, *Payback* DVD, Paramount Pictures, 2007.

84 James Toback, Director's Audiocommentary, *Fingers* DVD, Warner Home Video, 2002.

85 Douglas Keesey, *Paul Verhoeven*, ed. Paul Duncan, Köln: Taschen, 2005, p. 127.

86 Michael Caton-Jones, Director's Audiocommentary, *Basic Instinct 2* DVD, Sony Pictures, 2006.

87 Ibid.

88 Cameron Crowe, 'Introduction', *Vanilla Sky*, London: Faber and Faber, 2001, pp. vii–viii.

89 Cameron Crowe, Director's Audiocommentary, *Vanilla Sky* DVD, Paramount Pictures, 2002.

90 Ibid.

91 Ibid.

INDEX

A

Abre los ojos, 184–7
Acker, Sharon, 171
Akerman, Malin, 46
Alba, Jessica, 44
Allen, Joan, 89
Allen, Karen, 67
Almodóvar, Pedro, 149
Alonzo, John A, 19
Altman, Robert, 16
Amenábar, Alejandro, 184, 187
Amiel, Jon, 29
Amores Perros, 15, 141–3
Antonioni, Michelangelo, 104, 172
Arbogast, Thierry, 59
Arestrup, Niels, 178
Arquette, Patricia, 81
Arriaga Jordán, Guillermo, 141
Asano, Tadanobu, 143
Assayas, Olivier, 145–6
Audiard, Jacques, 178
Audran, Stéphane, 133
Aurenche, Jean, 133
Axelrod, George, 165, 168

B

Bad Education, 9, 12, 149–51
Badalucco, Michael, 57
Baldwin, Stephen, 36
Bale, Christian, 100
Ball, Nicholas, 74
Ballhaus, Michael, 189
Band Wagon, The, 13
Banderas, Antonio, 59
Bardem, Javier, 91
Barish, Leora, 182
Barnier, Luc, 145
Barray, Gérard, 184
Basic Instinct, 9, 15, 180–2
Basic Instinct 2, 13, 16, 182–4
Basinger, Kim, 39
Batman Begins, 101
Bauche, Vanessa, 141
Baudrillard, Jean, 43
Beals, Jennifer, 124, 127
Bean, Henry, 182
Beat That My Heart Skipped, The, 178–9
Beattie, Stuart, 91
Beebe, Dion, 91, 94
Bello, Maria, 174
Benacquista, Tonino, 178
Berling, Charles, 145
Berman, Henry, 171
Bigelow, Kathryn, 120–1
Black Dahlia, The, 62–4
Blade Runner, 12, 14, 16, 26–9

Blake, Robert, 81
Blanchett, Cate, 162
Blood on the Moon, 13
Blood Simple, 14–15, 51–3
Blue Steel, 13, 120–2
Blue Velvet, 14, 78–80
Bochner, Lloyd, 171
Body Heat, 9, 15, 24–6
Bonnot, Monique, 131
Boorman, John, 171, 173
Borde, Raymond, 10
Bould, Mark, 11
Bound, 15, 127–9
Bozzuffi, Marcel, 64
Brooks, Albert, 106
Brown, Clancy, 120
Brown, Jim, 176
Burman, Hans, 184
Buscemi, Steve, 54, 110
Busch, Niven, 155
Bush, George, Jr and Sr, 14–15
Byrne, Gabriel, 36

C

Cain, James M, 10, 155
Caine, Michael, 72, 100
Cameron, Paul, 91
Carballar, Luis, 141
Carlin, Paul, 76
Carlino, Lewis John, 117
Carter, Jim, 29
Cassidy, Joanna, 26
Caton-Jones, Michael, 182–4
Chandler, Raymond, 9–10, 29
Chang, Eileen, 151
Chapman, Michael, 22, 176
Chaumeton, Etienne, 10
Cheadle, Don, 106, 124
Chen, Joan, 151
Chen, Kelly, 189

Cheng, Sammi, 189
Chinatown, 9, 13–14, 19–21
Choi, Min-sik, 147
Chong, Felix, 189
Christie, Agatha, 31
Clean Slate, 133–5
Clifford, Graeme, 155
Clooney, George, 106
Coates, Anne V, 105
Coburn, James, 174
Coen, Ethan, 51, 54, 56–7
Coen, Joel, 51, 54–6, 58
Cohen, Gilles, 178
Colicos, John, 155
Collateral, 91–3
Condon, Richard, 165, 168
Contner, James, 67
Cooke, Tricia, 57
Core, Ericson, 174
Coup de torchon, 133–5
Cox, Brian, 89
Cox, Richard, 67
Coyote, Peter, 59
Crenna, Richard, 24
Criss Cross, 103, 105
Cromwell, James, 39
Cronenweth, Jordan, 26
Croupier, 74–6
Crowe, Cameron, 184, 187
Crowe, Russell, 39
Crudup, Billy, 46
Cruise, Tom, 91, 184, 188
Cruising, 15, 66–9
Cruz, Penélope, 184
Crying Game, The, 11–12, 15, 32–3
Curtis, Jamie Lee, 120

D

Dafoe, Willem, 69
Damon, Matt, 12, 162, 189, 193

Index

Danson, Ted, 24
Dark Knight, The, 14, 100–2
Davidson, Jaye, 32
Davis, Elliot, 103, 106
Dawson, Rosario, 44
De Battre mon coeur s'est arrêté, 178–9
de Bont, Jan, 180
De Niro, Robert, 22
De Palma, Brian, 16, 59, 61–3
de Rozas, María Elena Sáinz, 184
Deakins, Roger, 54, 57
Death Wish, 134
Decaë, Henri, 131, 160
Del Toro, Benicio, 44
Delon, Alain, 131, 160, 162
Delon, Nathalie, 131
Deming, Peter, 81, 83
Demme, Jonathan, 168–9
demonlover, 13, 16, 145–7
Departed, The, 12, 16, 189–90, 192–3
Dern, Laura, 78, 86–7
Detour, 10
Devane, William, 174
Devil in a Blue Dress, 12, 124–7
DeVito, Danny, 39, 105
Dexter, 13
Dhiegh, Khigh, 165
Diaz, Cameron, 184
DiCaprio, Leonardo, 12, 193
Dick, Philip K, 26, 81
Dickinson, Angie, 171
Dixon, Winston, 11
Do Androids Dream of Electric Sheep?, 26
D.O.A., 10
Dobbs, Lem, 108, 110
Dorn, Dody, 98
Double Indemnity, 9–10, 25, 61, 156
Douglas, Michael, 9, 180, 182
Dragnet, 13
Dunaway, Faye, 19

Dunham, Duwayne, 78
Duris, Romain, 178–9
Dzundza, George, 180

E

Echevarría, Emilio, 141
Eckhart, Aaron, 62, 100
Ekland, Britt, 72
El Shenawi, Ahmed, 136
Element of Crime, The, 136–8
Elise, Kimberly, 168
Elling, Tom, 136
Elliott, Alison, 103
Ellroy, James, 38, 62
Elmes, Frederick, 78
Elphick, Michael, 136
Ely, David, 117
Eszterhas, Joe, 180, 182

F

Fai, Lai Yiu, 189
Fancher, Hampton, 26
Fargo, 14–15, 54–6
Farina, Dennis, 106
Farmiga, Vera, 189
Farrell, Colin, 94
Farrow, Tisa, 176
Femme Fatale, 9, 13, 59–62, 63
Feuer, Debra, 69
Fichtner, William, 103
Fincher, David, 34
Fingers, 15, 175–7, 178–9
Fireworks, 138–41
Fishburne, Lawrence, 41
Flack, Sarah, 108
Fluegel, Darlanne, 69
Following, 13, 15, 96–8
Fonda, Peter, 108
Fong, Larry, 46

Fontaine, Stéphane, 133, 178
Forbrydelsens element, 136–8
Ford, Harrison, 26
Foreman, Jamie, 76
Foster, Jodie, 22
Foxx, Jamie, 91, 94
Francis-Bruce, Richard, 34
Frank, Scott, 105
Frankenheimer, John, 117, 120, 165, 168
Franklin, Carl, 124, 126–7
Freeman, Morgan, 9, 34
French Connection, The, 12, 64–6
French New Wave, 16
Friedkin, William, 64–6, 69, 71
Friedman, Josh, 62
Fuchs, Daniel, 103
Fujimoto, Tak, 124, 168

G

Gallagher, Peter, 103
Gambon, Michael, 29
Gandolfini, James, 13, 57
García Bernal, Gael, 141, 149–50
Gardiner, Greg, 122
Garfath, Mike, 74, 76
Garfield, John, 155, 157
Garnett, Tay, 155
Gazzo, Michael V., 176
Geer, Will, 117
Gégauff, Paul, 160
Georgaris, Dean, 168
Gershon, Gina, 127, 145
Get Carter, 72–4
Getty, Balthazar, 81
Getz, John, 51
Gibbons, Dave, 46
Gibson, Mel, 174
Gifford, Barry, 81
Gil, Mateo, 184
Gilda, 84

Giménez Cacho, Daniel, 149
Gislason, Tómas, 136
Glenn, Pierre-William, 133
Godard, Jean-Luc, 16
Goldenberg, William, 94
González Iñárritu, Alejandro, 141–2
Good Vibrations, 188
Goode, Matthew, 46
Graf, David, 122
Greenberg, Jerry, 64
Gregory, James, 165
Guerrero, Alvaro, 141
Gugino, Carla, 47
Guzman, Luis, 108
Gyllenhaal, Maggie, 100

H

Hackman, Gene, 12, 64
Haley, Jackie Earle, 47–8
Hammett, Dashiell, 10, 52
Hana-Bi, 138–41
Hannah, Daryl, 26
Hanson, Curtis, 38–9
Hardie, Kate, 74
Harring, Laura Elena, 83, 88
Harris, Mel, 122
Harris, Michael, 122
Harris, Naomie, 94
Harris, Thomas, 88
Hartnett, Josh, 62
Harvey, Laurence, 165
Hauer, Rutger, 26, 44
Haw, Alex, 96
Hayes, Terry, 173
Hays Code, 15
Haysbert, Dennis, 122
Hayter, David, 46
Hayworth, Rita, 84
Heal, Gareth, 96
Healey, Les, 74

Hedaya, Dan, 51
Hei, Pang Ching, 189
Helgeland, Brian, 38, 173–5
Hendry, Ian, 72
Henley, Barry Shabaka, 94
Henry, Gregg, 59, 174
Hepburn, Audrey, 188
Highsmith, Patricia, 160, 162
Hillier, Jim, 11
Hinds, Ciarán, 94
Hodges, Mike, 72, 74, 76–7
Hoenig, Dov, 88
Hoffman, Philip Seymour, 162
Homar, Lluís, 149
Honess, Peter, 39
Hopper, Dennis, 78
Howe, James Wong, 117
Hoy, William, 46
Hua, Tou Chung, 151
Hudson, Rock, 117, 119–20
Hunter, The, 171, 173
Huppert, Isabelle, 133
Hurt, William, 24
Huston, John, 19
Hutshing, Joe, 184

I
I'll Sleep When I'm Dead, 15, 76–8
Ichi the Killer, 15, 143–5
identities, 12, 95, 191
Infernal Affairs, 189–92
Infernal Affairs III, 192
INLAND EMPIRE, 9, 13, 86–8
Invasion of the Body Snatchers, 13
Irons, Jeremy, 86

J
Jack's Return Home, 72
Jackson, Samuel L, 113

Jacobs, Alexander, 171
James, Brion, 26
Javet, Françoise, 160
Jaynes, Roderick, 51, 54, 57
Jens, Salome, 117, 119
Jeong, Jeong-hun, 147
Ji, Dae-han, 147
Johansson, Scarlett, 57, 62
Jordan, Neil, 32

K
Kane, Bob, 100
Kang, Hye-jeong, 147
Kasdan, Lawrence, 24
Kearns, Bill, 160
Keitel, Harvey, 22, 110, 113, 176
Kellaway, Cecil, 155
Kershner, Mia, 62
Khondji, Darius, 34
Killing, The, 10
Kim, Sang-Beom, 147
King, Jaime, 44
Kingston, Alex, 74
Király, Istvan, 182
Kishimoto, Kayoko, 138
Kiss Me Deadly, 10
Kitano, Takeshi, 138–41
Kline, Richard H, 24
Knight, Esmond, 136
Koroshiya 1, 143–5
Kravetz, Carol, 124

L
L.A. Confidential, 9, 38–41
Lachman, Ed, 108
Laforêt, Marie, 160
Lai, Meme, 136
Lange, Jessica, 155, 158–9
Lansbury, Angela, 165

Lathrop, Philip H, 171
Lau, Andrew, 189
Lau, Andy, 189
Laura, 10
Law, Jude, 162
Lawrence, Robert, 176
Ledger, Heath, 100
Lee, Ang, 151
Lee, Jason, 184
Leigh, Janet, 165
Lenoir, Denis, 145
Leonard, Elmore, 105
Lera, Chete, 184
Leung, Tony, 151, 189
Lewis, Ted, 72
Li, Gong, 94
Limey, The, 108–10
Lindon, Lionel, 165
Ling, Wang Hui, 151
Littleton, Carol, 24, 168
Liu, Lucy Alexis, 174
Lo Bianco, Tony, 64
Loggia, Robert, 81
London, 30, 32, 72, 74, 76, 78, 96, 182
Lopez, Jennifer, 106
Los Angeles, 19, 27, 39, 62, 70, 91–2, 124, 171
Lost Highway, 16, 81–3
Lowry, Sam, 103
Lucas, Peter J, 86
Luis Alcaine, José, 149
Lust, Caution, 151–3
Lynch, David, 78, 81, 83, 86

M
MacLachlan, Kyle, 78
Macy, William H, 54
Madsen, Michael, 110
Mak, Alan, 189
Mala Educación, La, 149–51

Malahide, Patrick, 29
Malartre, Jean-Baptiste, 145
Maltese Falcon, The, 10
Mamet, David, 155, 159
Man Who Wasn't There, The, 9, 56–9
Manchurian Candidate, The (1962), 14, 165–8
Manchurian Candidate, The (2004), 14, 168–70
Manhunter, 12, 88–91, 95
Mann, Michael, 88, 90–3, 95
Marchand, Guy, 133
Marielle, Jean-Pierre, 133
Martínez, Fele, 149, 184
Marvin, Lee, 171, 173
Matrix, The, 11, 14, 16, 41–3
Maurette, Yo, 131
Mayersberg, Paul, 74, 76
McDormand, Frances, 51, 54, 56–7
McDowell, Malcolm, 76
McGehee, Scott, 122
McGill, Bruce, 91
McKay, Craig, 168
McKee, Gina, 74
McLeod, Joan, 131
McQuarrie, Christopher, 36
Melville, Jean-Pierre, 131–2, 172
Memento, 11–12, 98–100
Memento Mori, 98
Menke, Sally, 110, 112
Merrill, Dina, 122
Miami Vice, 93–5
Miike, Takashi, 143
Miller, Frank, 43, 45
Miller, Jim, 91
Minegishi, Nobuaki, 147
Minghella, Anthony, 161–2, 164
Mitchell, Eddy, 133
Mokri, Amir, 120
Monahan, William, 189
Moore, Alan, 46

Moore, Robin, 64
Morgan, Jeffrey-Dean, 9, 34, 47
Morrissey, David, 182
Mosley, Walter, 124
Moss, Carrie-Anne, 41, 98
Mou gaan dou, 189–92
Mulholland Dr., 83–6, 88
Muller, Robby, 69
Murch, Walter, 162
Murder of Roger Ackroyd, The, 31
Murphy, Brittany, 44

N
Nakashima, Marsha, 26
Naremore, James, 11
New York, 14, 22, 64–5, 67–8, 117–18, 120, 176, 189
Newhouse, David, 117
Newhouse, Rafe, 171
Newman, Barry, 108
Nicholson, Jack, 19, 155, 158, 189, 193
Nielsen, Connie, 145
Nimri, Najwa, 184
Noiret, Philippe, 133
Nolan, Christopher, 96, 98–100, 102
Nolan, Jonathan, 98
Noonan, Tom, 89
Noriega, Eduardo, 184
Nykvist, Sven, 155

O
O'Connor, Carroll, 171
O'Steen, Sam, 19
Oedipus, 21
Oh, Dal-su, 147
Oldboy, 147–9
Oldman, Gary, 100
Olmos, Edward James, 26
Omori, Nao, 143

Oota, Yoshinori, 138
Open Your Eyes, 184–7
Ormond, Julia, 86
Ortiz, John, 94
Osborne, John, 72
Osugi, Ren, 138
Ottman, John, 36
Out of Sight, 105–8
Owen, Clive, 44, 74, 76

P
Pacino, Al, 67
Pados, Gyula, 182
Pahm, Linh Dan, 178
Palminteri, Chazz, 36
Paltrow, Gwyneth, 34, 162
Pan, Kant, 32
Pang, Danny, 189
Pankow, Bill, 59, 62
Pankow, John, 69
Panorama of American Film Noir, A, 10
Pantoliano, Joe, 41, 98, 127
Park, Chan-wook, 147–9
Paterson, Bill, 29
Payback, 173–5
Paymer, David, 174
Pearce, Guy, 12, 39, 98
Pellegrin, Georges, 131
Pena, Elizabeth, 120
Penn, Chris, 110
Peoples, David, 26
Percy, Lee, 120
Pérez Unda, Fernando, 141
Périer, Francois, 131
Petersen, William, 12, 89
Petievich, Gerald, 69
Pfister, Wally, 98, 100
Phillips, Alastair, 11
Pieto, Rodrigo, 151
Pinkett Smith, Jada, 91
Pitt, Brad, 9, 34, 189

Plein soleil, 160–2
Plummer, Amanda, 113
Point Blank, 16, 171–3, 174–5
Polanski, Roman, 19, 21
Polito, Jon, 57
Pop. 1280, 133
Pope, Bill, 41, 127
Possessed, 13
Postlethwaite, Pete, 36
Postman Always Rings Twice, The (1946), 9–10, 25, 58, 155–8
Postman Always Rings Twice, The (1981), 155–6, 158–9
Potter, Dennis, 29
Presnell, Harve, 54
Preston, JA, 24
Preston, Trevor, 76–7
Prieto, Rodrigo, 141
Psenny, Armand, 133
Pullman, Bill, 81
Pulp Fiction, 15, 112–15
Purple Noon, 160–2
Pyne, Daniel, 168

R

Rafelson, Bob, 155
Rampling, Charlotte, 76, 182
Randolph, John, 117
Rea, Stephen, 32, 34
Reagan, Ronald, 15
Red Desert, 104
Red Dragon, 88
Red Harvest, 52
Red, Eric, 120
Reeves, Keanu, 41
Reservoir Dogs, 11, 13, 110–12, 113
Rey, Fernando, 64
Reymond, Dominique, 145
Rhames, Ving, 106, 113
Rhys Meyers, Jonathan, 76

Richardson, Julie, 32, 91
Rodriguez, Robert, 43
Roizman, Owen, 64
Rolf, Tom, 22
Romijn, Rebecca, 9, 59
Ronet, Maurice, 160
Ronin, The, 131
Rosier, Cathy, 131
Rossellini, Isabella, 78
Rourke, Mickey, 24, 44
Rubell, Paul, 91, 94
Ruffalo, Mark, 91
Ruskin, Harry, 155
Russell, Kurt, 184
Russell, Lucy, 96

S

Sabrina, 188
Salcedo, José, 149
Salfas, Stan, 103
Samurai, The, 15, 131–3
Sanderson, William, 26
Satô, Sakichi, 143
Scardino, Don, 67
Schamus, James, 151–2
Scheider, Roy, 64
Schoonmaker, Thelma, 189
Schrader, Paul, 14, 22–3
Schreiber, Liev, 168
Scorsese, Martin, 16, 22, 189, 192
Scott, John, 182
Scott, Ridley, 26, 28
Se, jie, 151–3
Se7en, 9, 13, 34–6
Seale, John, 162
Seconds, 117–20
Sekula, Andrzej, 110, 112
Seldes, Marian, 176
Sevigny, Chloë, 145
Shalhoub, Tony, 57

Shapiro, Melvin, 22
She's a Lady, 128
Sheen, Martin, 189
Shepherd, Cybill, 22
Shimamura, Yasushi, 143
Shimono, Sab, 122
Siegel, David, 122
Sigel, Newton Thomas, 36
Sikking, James, 171
Silver, Ron, 120
Simulacra and Simulation, 43
Sin City, 43–6
Sinatra, Frank, 165, 168
Singer, Bryan, 36
Singing Detective, The, 9, 29–31
Sizemore, Tom, 124
Skobline, Irène, 133
Sleep with Me, 161
Smith, Bud, 67
Smith, Lee, 100
Smith, Scott, 69
Snyder, Zack, 46, 48
Soderbergh, Steven, 103–6, 108, 110
Sonnenfeld, Barry, 51
Sopranos, The, 13
Sorvino, Paul, 67
Spacey, Kevin, 34, 36, 39
Spinotti, Dante, 39, 88
Squyres, Tim, 151
Staenberg, Zach, 41, 127
Stahl, Nick, 44
Stamp, Terence, 108
Stanwyck, Barbara, 9, 61, 125
Stark, Richard, 171, 173
Steadicam, 16
Steadman, Alison, 29
Stitt, Kevin, 174
Stockwell, Dean, 69, 78
Stone, Sharon, 9, 180, 182
Stormare, Peter, 54
Stott, Ken, 76
Strathairn, David, 39
Streep, Meryl, 168
Strong, Michael, 171
Stuck in the Middle with You, 111
Summertime, Summertime, 177
Sun, Alien, 143
Sunset Blvd, 10
Suschitzky, Wolfgang, 72
Suture, 15, 122–4
Suzman, Janet, 29
Swank, Hilary, 62
Sweeney, Mary, 81, 83, 86
Syms, Sylvia, 76

T

Talented Mr. Ripley, The, 14, 16, 162–5
Tarantino, Quentin, 110–12, 161
Tavernier, Bertrand, 133, 135
Taxi Driver, 14, 22–4, 48
Taylor, Noah, 184
Terajima, Susumu, 138
Thatcher, Margaret, 15
Theobald, Jeremy, 96
Theroux, Justin, 83, 86, 94
Thewlis, David, 182
Thompson, Jim, 133
Thornton, Billy Bob, 57
Thurman, Uma, 113
Tidyman, Ernest, 64
Tierney, Lawrence, 110
Tilly, Jennifer, 127
Tim Roth, 110, 113
To Live and Die in L.A., 16, 69–71
Toback, James, 175–6, 178
Toledo, Goya, 141
Toll, John, 184
Top Gun, 161
Tosar, Luis, 94
Touch of Evil, 10
Towne, Robert, 19, 21

Tracy, Don, 103
Travolta, John, 113
Tripplehorne, Jeanne, 180
Truffaut, François, 16
Trumper, John, 72
Tsang, Eric, 189
Tse, Alex, 46
Tsuchiya, Garon, 147
Tsukamoto, Shinya, 143
Turkel, Joe, 26
Turner, Kathleen, 24
Turner, Lana, 155, 157
Turturro, John, 69

U

Underneath, The, 103–5, 106
Unger, Deborah Kara, 174
Urioste, Frank J, 180
Usual Suspects, The, 36–8

V

Vanilla Sky, 16, 184–6, 187–9
Verhoeven, Paul, 180
Vernon, John, 171
Vertigo, 10
Voigt, Jon, 168
von Trier, Lars, 136–8
Vørsel, Niels, 136

W

Wachowski, Andy, 41
Wachowski, Larry, 41, 127–8
Wagner, Sidney, 155, 184
Wahlberg, Mark, 189
Walker, Andrew Kevin, 34
Walker, Gerald, 66
Walsh, M Emmet, 26, 51
Wang, Leehom, 151
Warren, Lesley Ann, 108
Washington, Denzel, 124, 168
Watchmen, 14, 46–9
Watts, Naomi, 83, 88
Weaving, Hugo, 41
Webster, Ferris, 117, 165
Wei, Tang, 151
Welfling, Juliette, 178
Wells, Jerold, 136
Westbury, Ken, 29
Westlake, Donald E, 171, 173
Whalley, Joanne, 29
Whitaker, Forest, 32
White Heat, 13
White, George, 155
Wiegmann, Don, 51
Willis, Bruce, 44, 113
Wilson, Ian, 32
Wilson, Patrick, 47
Wong, Anthony, 189
Wood, Elijah, 44
Wright, Bill, 29
Wright, Jeffrey, 168
Wyatt, Sue, 29
Wynn, Keenan, 171

Y

Yamamoto, Hideo, 138, 143
Yerkovich, Anthony, 93
Young, Sean, 26
Yu, Ji-Tae, 147

Z

Zabriskie, Grace, 86
Zaccaï, Jonathan, 178
Zsigmond, Vilmos, 62
Zuckerman, Lauren, 122

www.kamerabooks.com

→ Comprehensive and up to date look at cult director Dario Argento

→ Accessible introduction to a general readership of Argento's work which will also appeal to hardcore fan base

Dario Argento
James Gracey

The stylistic and bloody excesses of the films of Dario Argento are instantly recognisable. Vivid, baroque and nightmarish, his films lock violent deaths in a twisted embrace with an almost sexual beauty.

Hailed as one of horror cinema's most significant pioneers and the twentieth century's major masters of the macabre, Argento continues to create inimitable and feverishly violent films with a level of artistry rarely seen in the horror genre, influencing the likes of Quentin Tarantino, John Carpenter and Martin Scorsese. His high profile is confirmed with his role as producer on celebrated classics such as George A. Romero's *Dawn of the Dead* and Lamberto Bava's *Demons*. This Kamera Book examines his entire output, including his most recent film *Giallo*.

978-1-84243-318-8   £12.99

www.kamerabooks.com

→ An in-depth look at America's most renowned film auteur, including biographical detail

→ Covers all his film and television work, including the latest mystery feature *INLAND EMPIRE*, as well as his non-film projects

→ Discusses key themes, styles and choice of stars

David Lynch
Colin Odell & Michelle Le Blanc

Internationally renowned, David Lynch is America's premier purveyor of the surreal, an artist whose work in cinema and television has exposed the world to his highly personalised view of society. This book examines his entire works, from the cult surrealism of his debut feature *Eraserhead* to his latest mystery, *INLAND EMPIRE*, considering the themes, motifs and stories behind his incredible films.

In Lynch's world the mundane and the fantastical collide, often with terrifying consequences. It is a place where the abnormal is normal, where the respectable becomes sinister, where innocence is lost and redemption gained at a terrible price. And there's always music in the air. David Lynch is your guide to this other world… and this is your guide to David Lynch.

978-1-84243-225-9   £9.99

www.kamerabooks.com

→ Considers Blaxploitation from the perspective of class and racial rebellion, genre - and Stickin' it to the Man

→ Over 60 blaxploitation films reviewed and discussed

→ Fully up to date, including *Baadasssss* and *The Hebrew Hammer*

Blaxploitation Films
Mikel Koven

What is Blaxploitation? In the early 1970s a type of film emerged that featured all-black casts, really cool soul, R 'n' B and disco music soundtracks, characters sporting big guns, big dashikis, and even bigger 'fros, and had some of the meanest, baddest attitudes to shoot their way across our screens.

Blaxploitation Films considers Blaxploitation from the perspective of class and racial rebellion, genre - and Stickin' it to the Man, with over 60 Blaxploitation films reviewed and discussed. Sections include Blaxploitation horror films, kung-fu movies, Westerns and parodies and it is fully up to date, including *Baadasssss* and *The Hebrew Hammer* and covers the deaths of Isaac Hayes and Rudy Rae Moore.

978-1-84243-334-8   £12.99

www.kamerabooks.com

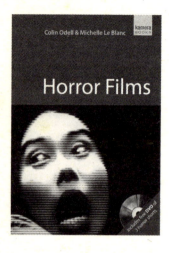

→ **Accompanying DVD features 3 horror shorts**

→ **Looks at renowned directors, including Wes Craven, John Carpenter, David Cronenberg, Dario Argento, Sam Raimi and Hideo Nakata**

→ **For horror aficionados and media or film students**

Horror Films

Colin Odell & Michelle Le Blanc

The Kamera Book of *Horror Films* takes you on a journey into the realm of fear. From horror cinema's beginnings in the late nineteenth century to the latest splatter films, from the chills of the ghost film to the terror of the living dead, there's more than enough to keep you awake at night.

There's a whole world of terror to explore – Spanish werewolves, Chinese vampires, Italian zombies, demons in Britain, killers in America, evil spirits in Japan.

This book offers a guide to key films, directors and movements, including *Dracula*, *Frankenstein*, *Scream*, *Halloween*, *The Sixth Sense*, *Ringu* and *Evil Dead*, and the more unusual *The Living Dead Girl*, *Rouge*, *Les Yeux sans Visage*, *Nang Nak* and *Black Cat*.

978-1-84243-218-1   £9.99